The Book of Life

VOLUME 1

God's Pioneers
The Patriarchs and Their Times

The Book of Life

VOLUME 1

God's Pioneers
The Patriarchs and Their Times

V. Gilbert Beers, Th.D., Ph.D.

THE ZONDERVAN CORPORATION

GRAND RAPIDS, MICHIGAN

The Book of Life

EDITORIAL STAFF

Managing Editor
Arlisle F. Beers

*Assistant Editors
and Staff Writers*
Janelle Diller
Elizabeth Gaines
Mavis Rice
Lawrence O. Richards

Proofreaders
Sandra Schultz
Mildred Tripp

Biblical Research
Merrill C. Tenney

Archaeological Research
Joyce Bartels

Rewrite
Barbara Rogasky

Research Assistants
Cynthia J. Beers
Janice L. Beers
Rebecca Gray Beers
Ronald A. Beers
Kathleen J. Cathey

ADMINISTRATIVE

Executive Director
Rex Jones
*Executive Vice President
Zondervan Book of Life*

ART AND DESIGN

Art Director
Chris Arvetis / *Rand McNally*

Designers
Chris Arvetis / *Rand McNally*
Vito De Pinto / *First Impression*

Principal Photographers
V. Gilbert & Arlisle F. Beers
Georg Gerster
Erich Lessing

Principal Artists
Ray App
Charles McBarron
Anne Ophelia Dowden
Tom Dunnington
Robert Korta
Marvin Nye
John Walter
Jack White

Production Coordinator
Arlean Vauthier / *Rand McNally*

The Book of Life was produced for
The Zondervan Corporation by Books for Living, Inc.

Color Separations by
Modern Litho, Grand Rapids, Michigan
and Mueller Color Plate Company, Milwaukee, Wisconsin

Library of Congress Catalog Card Number 80 – 50900
ISBN 0 – 310 – 79908 – 2

Manufactured in the United States of America
by Rand McNally & Company.

Illustration Acknowledgments

Location of illustration
on a given page is indicated by:
L–*left*, C–*center*, R–*right*,
T–*top*, B–*bottom*,
or combinations,
such as BLC–*bottom left center*,
and BL/C–*bottom left* and *center*.
Numbers refer to
pages within this volume.

Ray App: 84–85, 94, 96–97, 103, 105, 106L, 110, 111.
Eve Arnold, *Magnum*: 176T.
M. Bar-Am, *Magnum*: 104.
B. Barbey, *Magnum*: 24T, 169R.
Douglas Beers, *graphics*: 12–13, 22–23, 28–29, 36–37, 44–45, 54–55, 64–65, 72–73, 82–83, 92–93, 100–101, 108–109, 114–115, 122–123, 132–133, 140–141, 150, 151, 158–159, 166–167, 174–175, 182–183, 190–191.
V. Gilbert & Arlisle F. Beers: 14T/C, 15, 16, 17, 18, 19, 24B, 40T, 86T, 95B, 96L, 98, 99BR, 118, 119L/TR, 126, 128TR, 129, 130, 131, 135, 142T/C, 144, 145, 156BC/CR/BR, 157CL/BL, 160, 161R, 163, 165, 170T/C, 171, 172, 176BL, 178LC/B, 178–179, 184–185, 193, 194–195.
The Brooklyn Museum: 84L, 87L, 91TR.
R. Burri, *Magnum*: 14B, 86BL, 146–147, 154TR.
David Chenoweth: 70, 188.
E. Erwitt, *Magnum*: 38B.
L. Freed, *Magnum*: 125BR.
Georg Gerster: 32B, 34, 35B, 68–69, 77C, 79B, 116, 124, 128TL/B, 136TR, 136–137B, 137R, 148B, 149B, 154L/B, 156TC.
Jack Hagan: 117, 134, 143, 153, 161L, 162T.
C. Harbutt, *Magnum*: 38T, 119BR, 149T, 156TL.
E. Hartmann, *Magnum*: 38C, 87R, 95TR.
Robert Korta: 25, 30, 31, 33, 39, 40–41, 46, 48–49, 50R, 57, 58L, 67, 74–75B, 76–77T, 106R, 120–121, 180–181.

Erich Lessing, *Magnum*: 60, 61, 68B, 125TR, 142B, 147B, 148T, 155, 156BL, 156–157; Israel Museum: 186; Kunsthistoriches Museum, Vienna: 56; Louvre: 68T; Norbert Schimmel Collection, N.Y.: 59B.
Macmillan Publishing Co., Maps by Carta, Jerusalem: 20, 26, 27, 35T, 43T, 62, 90, 99L, 131TL, 138, 147T, 157R.
Metropolitan Museum of Art, New York: 76LC, 88B, 113, 136TL, 173L.
Inge Morath, *Magnum*: 32T, 74L.
Museum of Fine Arts, Boston: 82, 86BR, 112, 174.
National Aeronautics and Space Administration: 21, 58R, 63, 99TR.
The Oriental Institute, Chicago: 42, 50L, 51, 72, 75T, 76, 78, 79T, 80, 115, 121R.
M. Riboud, *Magnum*: 59T, 81T.
Steve Rockwell: 168–169, 177, 178T.
G. Rodger, *Magnum*: 102, 139R/C, 170B, 176BR.
M. Silverstone, *Magnum*: 66, 139L, 194BL.
Alan Sorrell, permission by Lutterworth Press, London: 81B.
The University Museum, University of Pennsylvania: 43B, 77B, 88T, 89, 91B, 150, 152, 162B, 173R.
John Walter: 184T, 186–187.
Jack White: 125L, 127, 192.
Stan Wilson: 47, 52–53, 71, 189, 197.

Preface:
The Patriarchs and Their Times

A small land
that changed
the world

From Dan to Beer-sheba was less than two hundred miles, a relatively small distance compared to other parts of the world. But between these two boundary markers of ancient Israel, approximately three-fourths of all Bible events took place. Here Abraham, Isaac, and Jacob moved about with their families, living much like the Bedouin of today. Here their descendants returned from a life of slavery in Egypt, conquering the land and gradually settling in it to build a new nation. Here also they dwelt for hundreds of years, at one time serving God faithfully, at another time turning from Him to worship idols and adopt the heathen customs of the people who had lived in the land before them.

From the land:
exile and
evangelism

From this land the people of Israel were taken into exile, to return later, weakened but determined to rebuild their faltering nation. In this land the people lived during the years of silence between the Old Testament and the New Testament, subject to one conquering empire after another. To this land a Savior came "in the fullness of time," fulfilling hundreds of years of prophecies concerning the Messiah. Almost all of His ministry focused on this small land, especially His crucifixion outside the city walls of Jerusalem. When it became apparent to Jesus' followers that He was the Messiah for whom they had waited, they went forth from this land to all parts of the Mediterranean world, telling both Jews and Gentiles the Good News.

Mesopotamia
and the Fertile
Crescent

The land of Israel, at some points in history known as the land of Canaan, lay at the western end of a great crescent of fertile land known as "the Fertile Crescent," an island of rich agricultural land in the midst of great deserts. At the eastern end of this crescent lay another center of early civilization, frequently called Mesopotamia. The Garden of Eden and the tower of Babel were thought to have been located in Mesopotamia. Abraham's hometown, Ur, was also here, near the southern tip, where Mesopotamia touched the Persian Gulf. Farther north in Mesopotamia, near Haran, Abraham's servant found Rebekah and took her back to Canaan to become Isaac's wife. Jacob came personally to this same place to find his bride, Rachel, as well as Leah, and there he served his father-in-law Laban for twenty years as a shepherd.

The events of this volume focus on "the beginnings," followed by great gaps of silence, then upon the lives of Abraham and Isaac, chosen by God to become the fathers of His people. No one is certain when the creation of the world or of man took place. But it is certain that a long period of time elapsed before Noah and the Great Flood. Some believe that after the Flood, approximately three thousand years went by before the Bible record picks up again with Abraham (Abram) and his migration to Canaan, with only a brief look at the events surrounding the tower of Babel and the names of a few early people. If that is so, the period of time between Noah and Abraham is greater than all of the following Bible history. *Events of this volume*

The lives of the early patriarchs, and the times in which they lived, are important in the panoramic sweep of God's dealings with His people. Through Noah, God perpetuated the human race. Through Abraham, Isaac, and Jacob, He perpetuated His covenant with His people. *The lives of the early patriarchs*

Noah, Abraham, Isaac, and Jacob are far from modern man in time and place. But their needs and human ways were much like ours today, and God's work in their lives is in many ways as contemporary as tomorrow. *The Bible: a bridge from yesterday to tomorrow*

Contents of Volume 1

The Book of Life Program

To many people the Bible is an ancient, mysterious book, written and compiled in lands and times far removed from modern life. The different cultures and customs of Bible people, and their lifestyles which contrast so sharply with ours, increase the mystery. Added to this is the difficulty of understanding certain words and phrases in the Bible text when it has been translated in yet another culture and time quite removed from today.

The daily lives of Abraham and Jacob, for example, were quite different from ours. They lived in tents, roamed the land as nomads, and cared for sheep, goats, and camels as a career. Family structures, government, technology, sociological systems, economy of the land, and many other facets of life are contrasted with modern culture.

To understand the record of God's relationship with people such as Abraham and Jacob, it is necessary to understand as much as possible about the way they lived and the way they thought. Without this, it is easy to view these people in our setting and thus we may not understand why they said or did what the Bible records.

THE BOOK OF LIFE helps you discover the Bible as a living book. It takes you back into the life and setting of these Bible people as though you were there. You see clearly where they lived and how they lived and what they said and did. In addition, you will discover the Bible as a readable book, clear and easy to understand, as well as enjoyable to read. Also, the Bible becomes a book with meaning for your life, for THE BOOK OF LIFE helps you discover from the Bible a richer life today and a better relationship with the Lord, the Author of the Bible.

The purposes of THE BOOK OF LIFE *program are:*

1. To help you return to Bible times and see things as they were, and thus understand the setting in which the people of the Bible lived and worked. You will see clearly many hard-to-understand things in the Bible. To accomplish this, hundreds of archaeological photos were gathered from the great museums of the world. Photo missions were taken to the holy land to gather first-hand information and pictures of the places which were important in the key events of the Bible. Thousands of hours of research focused on each facet of daily living in Bible times and the land of the Bible to assure an accurate presentation. Hundreds of original paintings and drawings were produced exclusively for

THE BOOK OF LIFE, making use of this research, and the best of current scholarship, to assure accuracy of content.

2. To introduce you to the people of the Bible as living people who had needs and problems similar to yours, even though they lived in times and circumstances different from yours.

3. To present the events of the Bible in the order in which they happened, helping them come alive through authentic paintings, drawings, and photos of places where they happened.

4. To help you discover how the Bible can bring meaning and purpose to your daily life, enriching your life as a believer.

5. To help you discover information concerning Bible events, people, places, and times which are interesting and informative to adults, yet easy for even a young child to understand.

6. To provide easy access to this wealth of material so that you may use it in many ways, such as personal Bible reading, Sunday school lesson preparation, group Bible study, higher education, or sermon preparation.

THE BOOK OF LIFE *program is arranged so that:*

1. All major events of the Bible are presented in a series of Bible readings, each chosen as the most useful length for you to read at one time. These readings are taken from the Bible itself, but are written in today's language.

2. Each reading is divided into three parts: an illustrated introduction, the Scripture in today's language, and a concluding section called *Bible for Daily Living,* which helps you apply the Scripture you have read to your life today.

3. A special feature, *The Bible Comes Alive,* accompanies each Bible reading, presenting an illustrated view of the Bible setting, or of something closely related to the Bible reading. This feature focuses on taking you back into the Bible pictorially so that you might see clearly how things were.

THE BOOK OF LIFE brings the Book, the Bible, into a close relationship with your life. You will see the Bible as few have seen it, and you will find the Bible a living book for your daily life.

In the Beginning

The first words of the Old Testament introduce us to the Bible's central message. "In the beginning, God." Behind the physical universe is a living Person. This Person is not only powerful, but is also magnificently creative. All the wonders and beauties of our world existed first in the imagination of God. Then He spoke, and they were created . . . from nothing. How great this God we meet in the Bible must be!

The Way the World Began
From Genesis 1:1–2:3

In the beginning God created the heavens and the earth. At first, the earth was a desolate waste, and a deep, brooding darkness covered the great empty places. Above it all, the Spirit of God hovered.

Then God sent forth a command over this wasteland. "Let light appear!" He ordered. The shadows scattered and light came upon the earth. God was pleased with the light and separated it from the darkness. When the light shone it was day, and when the darkness appeared it was night. This is how God made the first day, assigning a certain time for darkness and light to appear, separating them with evening and morning.

Then God ordered the waters of the earth to separate. The waters below became vast oceans, and the waters above became clouds and vapors. Separating the two was the great canopy of the heavens called the sky. By now, the end of the second day had come.

On the third day God caused the oceans to gather together into certain places, permitting the dry land to appear. God called the dry land Earth, and the gathering of the waters He called Sea. With this work God was pleased, for it was a good work.

"Now let the land be clothed with vegetation, seed-bearing

On the third day of creation God gathered together the waters of the earth and the dry land appeared.

plants and fruit trees that carry their seeds in the fruit, so that the seeds may continue to produce their own kind of plants." As God commanded these things, they happened, and the third day ended. With all of these things God was pleased.

God continued His work with this command: "Let bright lights appear in the sky to light the earth and separate the day from the night, to designate the seasons, the days, and the

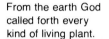

From the earth God called forth every kind of living plant.

years. Let them shine in the sky, giving light upon the earth."

It all happened as God commanded. He made two great lights, one to govern the day and the other to govern the night, and He also made the stars. God placed them in the canopy of the heavens, the sky, to shine upon the earth and to determine the times of light and darkness. God was pleased with these things, too. When He finished this work, the fourth day had ended.

On the fifth day, God gave another command. "Let the waters come alive with fish and sea creatures, and let birds of all kinds fly above the earth in the great canopy of the sky." So it happened the way God said. God made the waters come alive with all kinds of sea creatures, great and small, and placed the winged creatures in the sky. God was pleased with

all these things and blessed them, for they were good. "Multiply!" God told them all. "Fill the seas and the skies with your own kind!" When this work was finished, the fifth day came to a close.

Once again God spoke. "Let the earth produce every kind of living creature—cattle, reptiles, and the wild animals to roam the earth." So it happened. God made every kind of wild animal, cattle, and reptile, and God was pleased with the creatures that He had made.

Then God said, "Let Us make man to be like Us, and let him be in charge of all the fish of the sea, the birds of the sky, the cattle and the wild animals, and the reptiles that crawl upon the earth."

So God created man to be like Himself. In the image of the

God created fruit-bearing plants for food and flowering bushes to adorn the earth.

God called into being every kind
of living creature to inhabit
the earth, the seas, and the sky.

Maker, man and woman were made.

God blessed them and told them, "Multiply and fill the earth and bring it under your management. Rule over the fish of the sea, the birds of the air, and all living animals on the earth. For your food you will have all the seed-bearing plants and the trees with seed-bearing fruit, for I have given them to you. And to these creatures, I have given the plants to eat."

Then God looked upon His work and recognized how good it was. With this, the sixth day came to a close.

So the work of creation was finished, and the heaven and the earth were completed. On the seventh day God laid aside His work to rest. God blessed this seventh day and made it holy, for that was the day He had rested after all the work of His creation.

BIBLE FOR DAILY LIVING

Bible Memory
Genesis 1:1 is a must on every Bible memory list. It acknowledges God as the Creator and the heavens and earth as His creation. It therefore suggests that we are dependent on Him for life and sustenance.

Words and Meanings
"In the beginning God created." No man can do that. For God alone can make something from nothing, which is the act of creation. Man can construct something from something else, even from something else which is quite different. He can make a chair from wood which he obtained from a tree. But only God could make the tree. Man can combine hydrogen and oxygen to make water. Or he can break water into hydrogen and oxygen. But God alone can make earth's elements from nothing. He is the Creator, the only One Who can give life.

Personal Enrichment
God is creator. God is love. God is good. God is merciful. What else do you know about God? List all the qualities and attributes about God that come to mind. Look up "God" in a Bible dictionary and see which Scripture references tell about each of these. You may also find help in a topical Bible. When you have made a list of these various qualities, ask how man, made in the image of God, lives up to each of them. Then ask how you live up to them. This is a good test of the way we live daily in His image.

Something to Think About
Since we are made in the image of God, we should reflect His qualities, as mentioned above. Think about these questions: Do others see the qualities which God has reflected daily in us? Do others seeking God find our lives pointing to Him? If someone spoke of godly persons, would he think of us? How can we reflect His image more in our daily walk?

When God saw the beauty of all that He had created, He declared it good.

19

The Bible World

The world of the Bible was a relatively small world, especially compared to the world of today. If a large world map were stretched across these two pages, less than two square inches would represent the part known as the Bible world.

Within these two inches, the names of some nations have changed, while others remain the same as they have for thousands of years.

Names such as Jordan, Turkey, Iran, and Iraq would have been unfamiliar to the ancients. But Egypt has been a continuous nation for thousands of years. Canaan became Israel, which disappeared for two thousand years, to appear again in this generation.

Sumerians, Babylonians, Assyrians, Hittites, Philistines and many other nations and

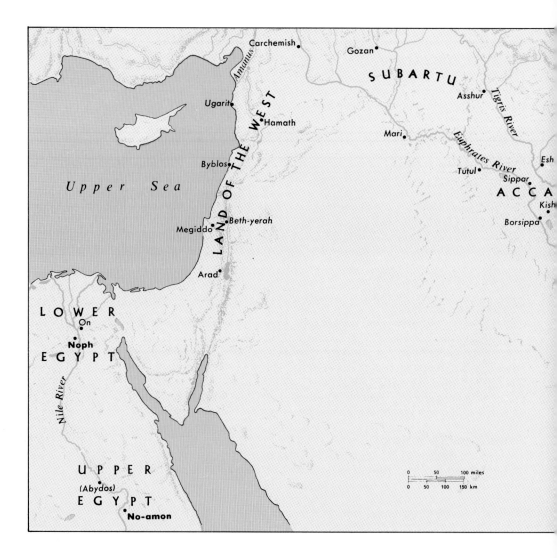

empires have gone down, to be raised again only by the archaeologist and historian.

Landmarks in the Bible world, rivers, mountains, lakes, and seas remain much the same as in Bible times. Some cities, such as Jericho and Damascus, have kept their names for thousands of years, even though the cities have changed greatly.

The world of the Bible was a relatively small world. But it has left a mark upon today's world far greater than its size would suggest.

The ancient Near East is often called "The Cradle of Civilization" because the earliest known empires were born in this part of the world. These great cultures grew up along the Nile River in the west and the Tigris and Euphrates Rivers in the east. The rivers were an important avenue of communication as well as an essential supply of water.

The Egyptians controlled the Nile River Valley for thousands of years without interruption. The natural barriers of desert and sea protected them from invaders. But Mesopotamia was open to conquerors from all sides. Sumer fell to the invading Amorites who overran the great centers of this ancient civilization.

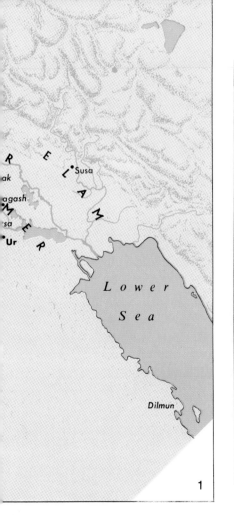

Life

The other planets in our solar system are sterile and empty. Our earth is joyfully alive with plants, trees, fish, birds, animals, and people. Life too is a gift from God. Living things, made to enjoy God's creation, are a vital testimony to His great love.

No rain cloud had yet darkened the sky. The dew on the ground watered the earth.

God planted the earth with every kind of food-bearing tree and flowering shrub for man to enjoy.

The Breath of Life
From Genesis 2:4-25

For some time after the Lord created the heavens and the earth there were no plants, because the Lord had not yet sent rain to water the land or placed man upon it to cultivate it. There was no moisture, except for the mists which rose from the ground and spread across the land.

Then from the dust of the ground the Lord fashioned a man's body and breathed into it the breath of life. And man became a living person.

Then the Lord planted a garden toward the east in a place called Eden, and in this garden He placed the man He had created. There were many varieties of trees in the garden, all beautiful and filled with good fruit. In the middle of the garden were two unusual trees. One was the tree of life. The other, the tree that helps one know good from evil.

A river flowed out of Eden through the garden, watering the plants and trees. As it left the garden, the river divided into four branches. One branch was called Pishon, which flowed through the land of Havilah. This land was known for its fine gold, bdellium, and onyx stone. The second branch of the river, called Gihon, flowed around the land of Cush. The third, the Tigris, flowed east of Assyria. The fourth branch was named Euphrates.

The Lord placed the man He had made in the garden of Eden to care for it. "You may eat all you wish from any tree in the garden, except from the tree that helps you know good from evil," the Lord said. "If you eat the fruit of that tree, you will certainly die."

Then the Lord said, "Man should not live in the garden alone. I will make someone to help him."

From the ground the Lord created the animals to roam the fields and the birds to fill the skies. He brought all these creatures before the man so that he could name them, for the Lord gave that responsibility to him. Thus the man gave each animal and bird its name. But still the man Adam did not have a helper.

Then the Lord caused a deep sleep to come upon the man. While he slept, the Lord removed one of his ribs and healed the opening from which it came.

From the rib the Lord fashioned a woman and brought her to the man. "This is one of my bones and part of my flesh," said the man. "She will be called woman, for she was taken from man."

This is why a man shall leave father and mother and become one flesh with his wife. And the man and woman were both naked, but they were not ashamed.

God made Adam His partner in creation. The Lord formed the animals and brought them to Adam to see what the man would name them.

BIBLE FOR DAILY LIVING

Bible Truth in Action

Most people have a greater appreciation for life when it seems that life is almost over. Thus, a threat to life, or a recognition of its brevity, heightens its value to us. Perhaps that is because we tend to value most what we have least. A young person in the full bloom of life sometimes eats and sleeps as though life has no limit and the body which houses life has no value. With age comes a greater recognition of life's limitations and brevity. The wise person recognizes life's brevity and value, however, no matter how old that person is. The wise person also recognizes life's beginning and its end—its origin and its eternal destiny. That recognition attaches a value to life which is far greater than silver or gold. So, in search of wisdom, we approach this reading with reverence, for it is a true record of life's origin.

Words and Meanings

The word "breath" has many meanings, among them "respiration, which is life." When a person stops breathing, he stops living. With the first breath, a baby begins life. God breathed His breath, and thus His life, into the first man's body, and life began. This was more than a secondary breathing, as in artificial respiration, which merely sets the lifeless person's breathing mechanism to work again. God's breathing into man was the impartation of original life—life that had never been there before. His breath also sustains life. Thus, in wisdom we pray to Him, "Breathe on me, breath of God. Fill me with life anew." As He began life with His breath, so He sustains it in the same manner.

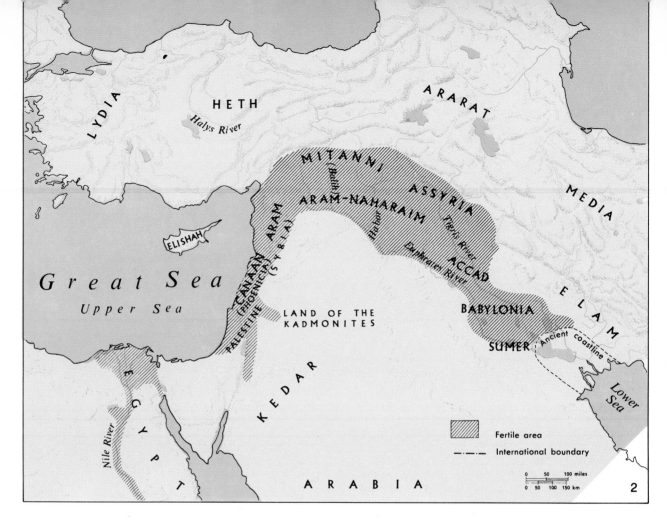

The Fertile Crescent

Rugged mountains, far-reaching expanses of desert, and lonely wilderness consume thousands of miles of the Middle East. This is land which stubbornly resists settlement. Cities and villages, flocks and herds, and the people who care for them need water. Farmers and vineyard keepers need not only water, but fertile soil in which to plant their crops. The wilderness has little of either water or fertile soil.

But in the midst of this vast stretch of lonely land there is a great crescent of water and fertile soil. On a map of the world, this crescent of rich land may seem small, but it stretches for about a thousand miles.

Since this great arc of land was a fertile, crescent-shaped plot of land in the midst of the wilderness, it was often referred to as "the fertile crescent."

The soil of the fertile crescent was capable of producing food for growing populations, often clustered in or around earliest cities and their satellite villages. Wheat, barley and beans grew in abundance and cattle thrived on the plentiful pasture.

Thus it is not surprising that earliest civilizations spread along this fertile land, stretching from the Persian Gulf on the eastern side to the land of Canaan, later Israel, on the west.

The crescent was watered by some of the great rivers of the Bible—the Tigris, Eu-

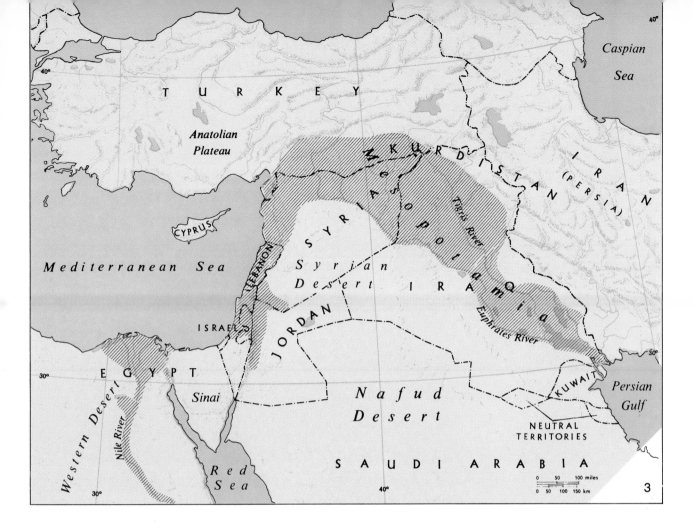

The shaded portions of the maps above represent the fertile areas of the Middle East.

phrates, Orontes, and the Jordan. In addition, there were numerous lesser-known rivers. These rivers not only provided water for fields and vineyards, pastures and gardens, but offered travel and communications as well. They connected the isolated cities of the Mesopotamian plain, and helped create one of the earliest great empires.

Here the Sumerians, early empire builders, reached great heights of power and achievement. They built great cities and developed the earliest known system of writing.

Abraham's roots came from the Sumerians, for he grew up in their important city of Ur, near the southeastern base of the fertile crescent. In his pilgrimage to Canaan, he moved along the fertile crescent, and not straight west across the hostile desert.

Sumerian culture was more advanced in early Bible history than the culture of Canaan and Syria to the west. It was not until many years later, when the Israelites conquered Canaan and settled the land, that the western side of the fertile crescent developed its resources and gained its place in world power.

The shaped of the Fertile Crescent remains unchanged although new nations have replaced the old empires.

Two Trees

The Bible tells the story of human failure as well as of God's love. Frequently, a tree plays an important part. Here we read of a forbidden tree, and of the disobedience which brought sin and death into our world. Later in the Bible we will read of a tree called "the cross," where God gave the gift of eternal life. Even in this tragic first story of sin, we catch a glimpse of a tree of life.

Forbidden Fruit

From Genesis 3

Of all the creatures God made, the serpent was the most cunning. "Did God command you not to eat any of the fruit in the garden?" he asked the woman one day.

"Oh, no," the woman answered. "Only the fruit from the tree in the center of the garden is forbidden. God warned us not to eat that fruit or even touch it, for if we do we will die."

"God knows that isn't true," said the serpent. "He knows that your eyes will be opened when you eat that fruit, and then you will have His power to know good from evil."

The fruit looked beautiful. The woman was sure that it would be delicious, and convinced by the serpent that it would make her wise, she picked some of the fruit and ate it. She also gave some to her husband, and he ate it, too.

But as soon as the man and woman had eaten the fruit, they realized that they were naked, and they were ashamed. So they sewed fig leaves together to make clothing to cover themselves.

In the cool of the day the man and woman heard the sound of the Lord walking in the garden, and they were afraid. They quickly hid themselves among the trees of the garden.

"Where are you?" the Lord called to the man.

"When I heard You coming I hid, because I was ashamed for You to find me naked," the man answered.

"Who told you that you were naked?" the Lord asked. "Have you eaten the forbidden fruit from the tree that I warned you not to touch?"

"It was the woman You gave me who brought the fruit to me," the man argued. "Then I ate it."

"Why did you do that?" the Lord asked the woman.

"The serpent deceived me," the woman answered.

Then the Lord spoke to the serpent and told him of the punishment He was sending:

> "Because of what you have done,
> You are cursed more than all animals,
> Both the wild and tame animals of the earth.
> As long as you live
> You will crawl on the ground,
> Making your way through the dust.
> I will cause you and the woman
> And your offspring and hers
> To be enemies.

The fruit of the Tree of Knowledge hung temptingly within Eve's reach. With the words of the serpent whispering in her ear, the forbidden fruit seemed more desirable than all the pleasures of Eden.

The source of the Tigris River
is high in the Zagros mountains
of Kurdistan. It winds its way over
twelve hundred miles to its mouth at
the Persian Gulf. Green fields and
forests of palm trees line its banks.

> While you strike at his heel,
> He will crush your head."

The Lord also spoke this punishment to the woman:

> "I will bring great pain to you
> When you give birth to children.
> Yet you will still desire your husband
> And he will rule over you."

To Adam God gave this punishment:

> "Because you listened to your wife
> And ate the forbidden fruit—
> The fruit which I warned you
> Not even to touch,
> Cursed is the ground because of you;
> You will labor and struggle
> To earn a living from it
> As long as you live.
> While you sweat and toil
> To grow plants to eat,
> The soil will also grow
> Thorns and thistles for you.
> Until the day you die
> You will sweat and toil
> To earn your daily bread.
> Then you will return to the ground
> From which you were taken;
> For you were made of dust,
> And to dust your body will return."

The man named his wife Eve, which meant "The One Who Gives Life," for she became the mother of all people who were born on earth. The Lord made clothing from animal skins for Adam and Eve to wear.

"The man has become like one of Us," the Lord said, "because he knows good from evil. Now he must not eat from the tree of life and live forever in this condition."

Therefore the Lord drove the man out of the garden of Eden and made him cultivate the soil from which he was made. At the eastern entrance to the garden of Eden the Lord stationed cherubim and a flaming sword which turned in every direction, guarding the path to the tree of life.

The flash of the angel's sword cut off the entrance to Eden. Because they disobeyed God's command, Adam and Eve were driven out of the garden.

BIBLE FOR DAILY LIVING

Bible Quiz

The following Bible quiz reviews the account of creation, as given in the preceding three readings:

1. See how many of the following you can match with the seven days of creation:

   a. fish and birds b. dry land and plants c. heavens and earth d. light and darkness e. sun, moon, and stars f. man and animals g. rest

2. The garden where the Lord placed the first man and woman was called

   a. Cush b. Havilah c. Eden

3. The river which left the garden divided into four branches, called

   a. Gihon b. Pishon c. Havilah d. Cush e. Tigris f. Euphrates

4. Whom did the serpent tempt first?

   a. Adam b. Eve

5. Who ate the forbidden fruit first?

   a. Adam b. Eve

6. Eve was named by

   a. Adam b. God

7. The animals were named by

   a. Adam b. Eve c. God

Answers: 1a(5), b(3), c(2), d(1), e(4), f(6), g(7); 2c; 3a,b,e,f; 4b; 5b; 6a; 7a

Prayer Pointers

I pray not to be spared temptation, but to receive strength to resist it. I pray not to be spared trouble, but to have You by my side to guide me safely through it.

At the far right, the waters of the Tigris and Euphrates Rivers meet in a single stream before emptying into the Persian Gulf.

Mesopotamian marsh dwellers preserve their ancient way of life in the neighborhood of Eden. Marsh reed huts (above and at right) sit on individual islands surrounded by shallow swamp water.

The Garden of Eden

Almost anyone who reads the account of Adam and Eve wonders about the Garden of Eden. What was it like? What kind of plants grew there? How large was it? Where was it located? What has become of it?

The Bible is the only guidebook to Eden, and it gives only a few clues. The Genesis account says the river that flowed out of the garden divided into four branches that became the Tigris, the Euphrates, the Pishon and the Gihon.

Two of these rivers are known today. The Tigris and Euphrates flow through the modern countries of Iraq, Syria and Turkey.

But the Pishon and the Gihon remain a mystery. Some have suggested that they are branches of the Nile River in Egypt. Others say that they are smaller branches of the Tigris and Euphrates. The exact location remains a secret.

What has happened to this marvelous garden? Nobody knows. Some believe it withered and died when God expelled Adam and Eve. Others say it was destroyed by the waters of the Great Flood in Noah's time. Some think the garden may still exist, hidden from men's eyes.

Many have searched for Eden, but no one has found the exact location. However, it would seem that the juncture of the Tigris and Euphrates Rivers may be close. The pictorial material on these pages shows what that area is like today.

For modern man, the importance of Eden does not lie in its foliage or its location, but in the events that happened there and the lessons to be learned from them.

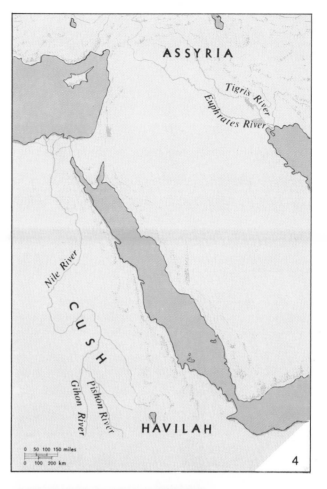

At left, a garden planted by human hands flourishes in the rich Mesopotamian soil. The walled house and orchard is a typical scene in rural Iraq. The map above shows the area where the Garden of Eden is thought to be, near the Tigris and Euphrates Rivers. Nobody knows where the Pishon and Gihon Rivers are, though some believe them to be in Egypt, as shown above.

The Sinister Shadow

God had warned Adam and Eve. The day you eat of the forbidden tree you shall surely die. The proof that death did come is seen in following generations. Cain murdered his own brother. Lamech broke God's pattern for marriage, and took murderous revenge. Through the ages hatred, anger, crimes and wars show the unmistakable mark. The sinister shadow of sin and death can still be seen.

These Arab farmers work the land with simple, handmade tools much like those their ancestors used in Bible times.

The work of the shepherd is an honored and ancient occupation. Abel, Adam's second son, was the first herdsman.

After he was driven out of Eden, Adam struggled to grow food from the stony ground. Like his father, Cain became a farmer.

A Marked Man

From Genesis 4

Eve gave birth to a son and named him Cain, saying, "I have brought forth a man with the Lord's help. Later she had another son and named him Abel. Abel became a shepherd and Cain became a farmer.

One day Cain brought some of his crops to the Lord as an offering. Abel also brought an offering to the Lord—the best and fattest of his flocks. The Lord accepted Abel and his offering but not Cain and his offering. So Cain's face clouded with anger and hate.

"Why are you angry and hateful?" the Lord asked. "If you please Me, your face will be radiant again. If you do not, sin crouches at the door, waiting to conquer you. But you can have victory over it."

Then Cain spoke with his brother Abel. "Let's go to the fields," he urged. When they arrived, Cain attacked Abel and murdered him.

But the Lord said to Cain, "Where is your brother Abel?"

"I don't know," Cain answered. "Must I take care of my brother?"

"What have you done?" the Lord persisted. "Your brother's blood cries out to me from the ground. You must leave the ground where you murdered your brother, for it is defiled by his blood and you are cursed by it. You will never harvest crops on this land again no matter how hard you work to farm it. You will always remain a fugitive, wandering about on the earth."

"How can I bear such great punishment?" Cain cried out. "You have driven me from my land, to hide from Your face. I will remain a fugitive to wander about on the earth. Whoever finds me will try to kill me."

"No, that will not happen," the Lord answered. "Whoever tries to kill you will receive seven times your punishment."

Then the Lord put a mark on Cain so that anyone who found him would not kill him. Cain left his land and the Lord's presence to live in the land of Nod, east of Eden.

Cain and his wife had a son and named him Enoch. When Cain founded a city, he named it Enoch, after his son.

Enoch became the father of Irad, Irad became the father of Mehujael, Mehujael became the father of Methushael, and Methushael became the father of Lamech.

Lamech married two wives, named Adah and Zillah. Adah gave birth to a son named Jabal. He became the ancestor of

Cain was jealous of his brother because God accepted Abel's sacrifice but rejected his own offering. With hatred brewing inside him, Cain plotted to kill his brother.

those who live in tents and raise cattle. His brother was Jubal, the ancestor of those who play the harp and flute.

Zillah had a son named Tubal-cain, who forged instruments of bronze and iron. Tubal-cain's sister was Naamah.

Lamech said to his wives one day:

"Adah and Zillah, listen to me;
You, my wives, hear what I say:
I have killed a man who wounded me
A young man who attacked me.
If the punishment for killing Cain
Is seven times greater than his own,
The punishment for killing me
Is seventy-seven times greater than mine."

Adam and Eve had another son and named him Seth, for Eve said, "God has given me a child in Abel's place, for Cain murdered him." Seth later had a son and named him Enosh. While Enosh was alive people began to call upon the name of the Lord.

In the open fields near the site of ancient Antioch, a tribe of nomads care for their camels and flocks, a reminder of the times of the patriarchs.

BIBLE FOR DAILY LIVING

Bible Truth in Action

Two men brought offerings to the Lord. One came with his heart open to the Lord. His offering was received. The other came with his heart filled with anger and hate. His offering was rejected. "If you please Me, your face will be radiant again," the Lord told the second man, Cain. But Cain proved his desire not to please the Lord by fulfilling his anger and hatred, and murdering his brother. A heart pleasing to God is an offering acceptable to Him. A heart displeasing to Him is an offering which He cannot accept. The offering in our hands is far less than the heart with which we bring it.

Personal Checkup

Apply what you have learned in this reading to the following questions: Would the Lord rather receive a dollar cheerfully given or a thousand dollars grudgingly given? When we bring an offering to the Lord, which is the true offering—what we carry in our hands or what we bring in our hearts?

Prayer Pointers

Receive my offering, O Lord; not merely what I bring in my hands, but even more, what I bring in my heart.

Startled by the voice of God, Cain guiltily drops his murder weapon. The Lord punished his crime with a curse on all his attempts to farm the land. From now on he must be a fugitive and a wanderer.

Families of Nations

Cain and Abel were the oldest sons of Adam and Eve, but they were not the only children born to the first couple. Seth, born after Abel's murder, was followed by many brothers and sisters. The Bible does not give their names, but it is known that these children married and had children of their own. As generation followed generation, the family multiplied and formed small groups called clans. Many clans joined together to become tribes, and the tribes eventually grew into nations.

The Bible does not trace all of Adam's descendants. Only the families of Cain and

The wide-eyed stare of a Sumerian priest is typical of the small statues of this period.

This fragment from a Sumerian relief captures scenes from everyday life in the ancient world.

A congregation of stone statuettes offered prayers before the silent image of Abu, one of a multitude of gods worshiped by the ancient Sumerians.

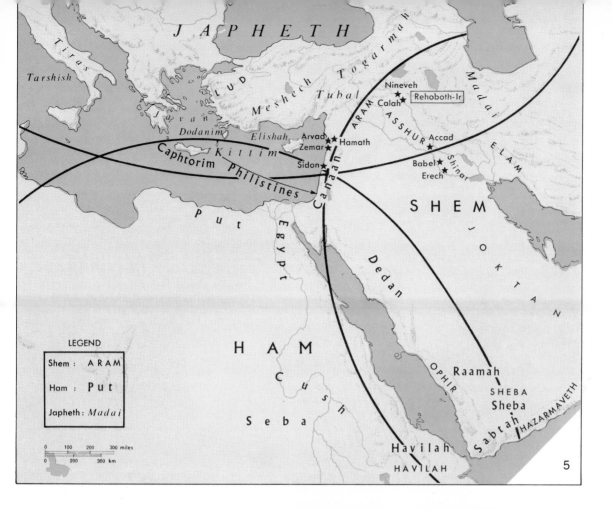

The three great branches of the human family descended from Adam's sons spread out from their focal point in the Holy Land.

Seth are included in the Book of Genesis. Even those histories have been shortened by leaving out the names of many family members. Several generations may be omitted between each step in the family tree. The word "begat," which means "to become the father of," can also mean "to be the ancestor of."

Cain was the founder of the first city in history, and the ancestor of the earliest musicians and metalworkers. Although he was originally a farmer, his descendants included the early herdsmen who lived in tents.

Cain's descendants perished in the Great Flood, but Seth's line was preserved through Noah. Shem, Noah's youngest son, became the ancestor of Abraham. From Abraham the line of Seth stretched to David. Eventually it reached its climax many centuries later in the birth of Jesus Christ.

The Sumerians were descended from Shem, the father of Mesopotamia and Arabia. At left, two votive statues preserve the likeness of men who lived more than five thousand years ago.

The Ark

The dark shadow cast by sin deepened as mankind turned completely to evil. God determined that such corruption must be cleansed. He chose a great destroying flood. But one man, Noah, had not followed the ways of sin. God told Noah and his family to build a great floating ark, in which they and many animals would be saved. God does punish sin. And He protects those who love good.

Two ancient medals here picture Noah's Ark and the great flood.

A Man Who Found Favor

From Genesis 6:1 – 7:10

As the population of the world increased, some of God's created beings began to notice the beautiful women of the world. In time these sons of God married the daughters of men, which displeased God.

"My Spirit will not remain with man forever, for he is evil," the Lord said. "I will permit mankind to live another hundred and twenty years."

In these early days giants lived in the world. Later, as the sons of God mated with the daughters of men, their children became the mighty men about whom so many stories are told.

God watched the wickedness of the people grow worse until the entire direction of their lives was toward evil. This grieved God so much that He was sorry He had created them.

"I will destroy all people from the earth," God said. "I will destroy even the animals, birds, and reptiles, for I am sorry that I have created them."

But Noah pleased God. He was a righteous man, the most perfect man who lived at that time. His three sons were Shem, Ham, and Japheth.

The world of Noah's time was very wicked, filled with violence. God saw how corrupt the world had become, for it was filled with evil.

"I will destroy all of the people of the world, for they are corrupt and violent," God told Noah. "I will wipe them from the face of the earth.

With the help of his three sons, Noah built the ark from God's instructions. The massive project took one hundred and twenty years to complete. When it was finished Noah was six hundred years old.

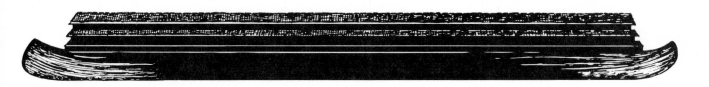

47

Two of each kind of animal that could not be eaten went into the ark. Fourteen of each kind of edible animal, and fourteen of each kind of bird went in.

"Make an ark, a great ship, of gopher wood; make rooms in it, and cover it with pitch inside and outside. Make it four hundred and fifty feet long, seventy-five feet wide, and forty-five feet high. Build an open window around the top part of the ark, about eighteen inches below the roof. Make three decks inside, and put a great door in its side.

"I will cover the earth with a flood which will destroy everything that breathes. But I will make a covenant with you and will keep you and your wife, and your three sons and their wives, safe inside the ark during the flood.

"You shall bring a male and female of each kind of animal, bird, and reptile into the ark with you to keep them safe during the flood. Store enough of the right kind of food in the ark so that you and the animals will have enough to eat."

And Noah did all that God commanded him.

At last the ark was built and the time for the flood had come. "You must enter the ark now with your family," God said to Noah, "for you alone are righteous. Take seven pairs of birds on the ark with you and seven pairs of animals which are acceptable for food and sacrifice, along with a pair of every other kind of animal, bird, and reptile so that life will continue after the flood. Seven days from now I will send rain upon the earth for forty days and forty nights, destroying all life on the earth."

And Noah did all that God commanded him.

When the flood came upon the earth, Noah was six hundred years old. He took his family into the ark with him—his wife, his three sons, and their wives. All of the animals, birds, and reptiles entered the ark with Noah in pairs, male and female, exactly as the Lord had commanded.

These club-shaped mallets
were the tools of an ancient
craftsman. Their broad, wooden
heads served as hammers.

BIBLE FOR DAILY LIVING

Bible Truth in Action

Two words stand out in this reading. "Wickedness" was a word used to describe the people whose entire direction in life was toward evil. "Righteous" was a word used to describe one man who pleased God. Associated with the word "wickedness" were the words "evil," "violence," "corrupt," "lust," and God's reaction, "destroy." Associated with the word "righteous" were the words "pleased God," "perfect," and "exactly as the Lord had commanded." God's reaction to the righteous man was to spare him from destruction.

Personal Enrichment

As you read various portions of the Bible, look for words, people, actions, attitudes, and punishments associated with evil. List them in a column parallel to another one with words, people, actions, attitudes and rewards associated with righteousness. The two divide dramatically, offering each person a striking choice.

People Profiles

From this reading, and the ones to follow, make a profile of Noah the man. List qualities which characterize the man. Look up "Noah" in a Bible dictionary to see how your profile compares. Ask the following questions: (1) Did Noah always please God or were there times when he did things displeasing to Him? (2) How long did Noah live before and after the Flood? (3) Were all of Noah's sons godly men, or did one seem to have a problem?

Something to Think About

If you were asked to work for a hundred and twenty years to make a great boat in a desert, what would your reaction be? How would you react if all your friends and neighbors ridiculed the work? The test of obedience is not always related to how clearly we understand God's instructions, but often to how comfortable we feel in carrying out those instructions. True obedience is doing anything God wants.

ROMAN MERCHANTMAN
100-180 FT.

The Ark

The ark was a wonder of ancient shipbuilding. It was far greater than other ships that would be built for centuries to come. Its purpose was simple, to house and protect people and animals throughout the period of the Great Flood.

The ark was designed to ride the waves of the rising flood without capsizing. It was six times longer than it was wide—a ratio used by modern shipbuilders.

Some features necessary for ships were missing in the ark. Since speed and direction were not necessary, the prow did not need to be curved. Nor did the ark need sails or rudder. The ark was three stories high, made of gopher wood and sealed with pitch. No wonder it took a hundred and twenty years to build it!

SANTA MARIA
77 FT.

CLAREMONT - 149 FT.

NOAH'S ARK - 450 FT.

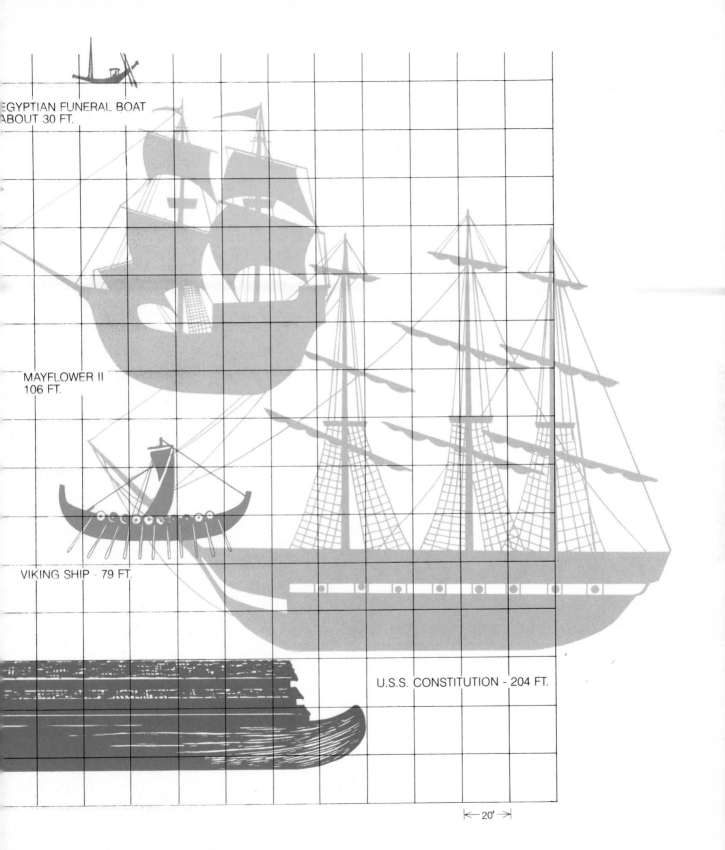

EGYPTIAN FUNERAL BOAT
ABOUT 30 FT.

MAYFLOWER II
106 FT.

VIKING SHIP - 79 FT.

U.S.S. CONSTITUTION - 204 FT.

|← 20' →|

53

New Life

When the crushing flood of waters receded, all people and animals had been destroyed. But fresh life began to spring up from the ground. One year after entering the ark, Noah and the animals with him would emerge. They would find a fresh new world in which to live.

The Great Flood
From Genesis 7:11–8:22

On the seventeenth day of the second month, when Noah was six hundred years old, the heavens opened and the rains poured forth from them. From the depths of the earth great fountains of water gushed out. The waters poured out on the earth for forty days and forty nights.

On the day the rains began, Noah and his wife and their sons, Shem, Ham, and Japheth, and their wives went into the ark. With them went the birds, the reptiles, and the wild and domestic animals. These creatures came into the ark in pairs, male and female, as God had commanded. When everyone and everything was on board, God closed the great door of the ark.

For forty days the waters continued to flood the earth, rising above the ground and lifting the ark with it. As the waters rose higher and higher, the ark floated safely on the surface of the flood, rising more than twenty feet above the peaks of the highest mountains.

In this great flood all living creatures of the earth perished, birds, wild and domestic animals, reptiles, and people, everything that had the breath of life in it. God destroyed all living creatures except Noah and his family.

For a hundred and fifty days the waters remained on the earth. Throughout that time God never forgot Noah and the animals in the ark with him. When the rains and torrents of waters ceased, God sent a wind across the earth and the floods began to go down. The waters receded slowly. On the seventeenth day of the seventh month the ark came to rest on the mountains of Ararat.

The waters continued to go down until the first day of the tenth month, when the peaks of the mountains became visible. Forty days later Noah released a raven through a window of the ark. The raven flew about until there was a place to land.

Then Noah released a dove to find out if the water was gone. But the dove could not find any place to rest, because water still covered the earth; so she returned to the ark.

Seven days later Noah released the dove again. Toward evening she returned with a freshly picked olive leaf in her beak. Then Noah knew that the water was gone from the earth at last. He waited another seven days to send out the dove again, and this time she did not return.

The world that existed before the Flood was washed away by the rising water. Only Noah and those who were with him in the ark were saved from the destruction of mankind. Above: the profile of an ancient Semite, a descendant of Shem.

On the first day of the first month, when Noah was six hundred and one years old, the water dried from the earth. Noah removed the covering from the ark and found that the water was gone. By the twenty-seventh day of the second month the ground was dry.

God spoke to Noah at this time. "Leave the ark with your wife, your sons, and their wives. Bring with you all the birds, animals, and reptiles so that they may reproduce in great numbers on the earth."

Noah obeyed the Lord and left the ark with his sons, his wife, and his sons' wives. Every animal, reptile, and bird left the ark with him in pairs and families.

Then Noah built an altar to the Lord, offering on it some of each kind of clean animal and bird. These he presented to the Lord as burnt offerings.

The Lord was pleased with the fragrant offering and made a promise to Himself. "Never again will I curse the ground because of man's sin, although he is wicked from the days of his youth. I will never again destroy every living thing, as I have done at this time.

"As long as the earth remains,
Seedtime and harvest,
Cold and heat,
Summer and winter,
Day and night
Shall never cease."

After the rains had ended Noah sent out a dove to search the earth for a sign of dry land.

Mount Ararat (as seen from space at right) is an ancient volcano in the eastern part of Turkey.

The heat of summer cannot melt the perpetual snowcap which covers the peak of Mount Ararat. According to tradition, this rugged mountaintop was the biblical Mount Ararat where Noah's ark came to rest.

An olive branch was the first sign that plant life was flourishing on the earth once more. The relief at left comes from the temple of Ramses II.

Gradually the dry land reappeared. As the Flood receded
the mountains emerged from the waters like islands
in a great sea.

BIBLE FOR DAILY LIVING

Bible Quiz
The period of time in the past three readings covers many hundreds of years. No one knows for sure how many. The following quiz, however, reviews the facts presented in the Bible account, however long it may have been:
1. Who was a farmer?
   a. Cain   b. Abel
2. Whose offering was acceptable to God?
   a. Cain's   b. Abel's
3. Which man murdered his brother?
   a. Cain   b. Abel
4. Adam and Eve had a third son, whose name was
   a. Enosh   b. Seth   c. Lamech
5. Which of the following was not a son of Noah?
   a. Enosh   b. Ham   c. Japheth   d. Shem
6. How old was Noah when the Flood came?
   a. 350   b. 600   c. 750
7. How many people were on the ark?
   a. 4   b. 6   c. 8
8. How many of each species of bird were on the ark?
   a. 2   b. 7   c. 14

Answers: 1a, 2b, 3a, 4b, 5a, 6b, 7c, 8c

Prayer Pointers
Like Abel, may I be acceptable to You, O Lord. And like Noah, may it be said of me that I have pleased You because I have walked righteously before You.

The Ancient Near East

Bible history does not flow generation to generation throughout ancient times. Instead, there are gaps, or periods of silence, filled only by ancient history and archaeology.

For example, the account of Abraham, which begins toward the end of Genesis 11, took place about 2000 B.C. All of the rest of the Old Testament happened within the next two-thousand-year span. Probably an even greater period of history took place between the early part of Genesis 11 and Abraham's story in the latter part of Genesis 11. It is estimated that as much as twenty-five hundred years went by between the Tower of Babel and Abraham. As much as three

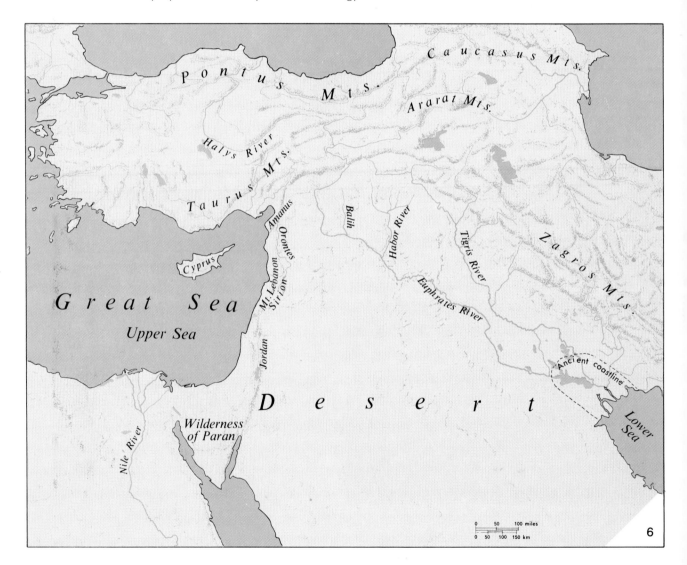

thousand years went by between Noah's life and Abraham's. In either case, it is more time than has gone by since the coming of Christ, or more time than the entire balance of the Old Testament record after Genesis 11.

The world's history in these early years focused on a crescent-shaped stretch of rich land known as the fertile crescent (see pages 26-27). Above the crescent was a vast area of mountains and below it an equally vast area of desert.

For the most part, early mankind avoided the mountains and deserts and built his civilization in the broad river valleys of the fertile crescent and in Egypt. Toward the eastern side of the crescent Mesopotamian culture arose. Toward the west, Canaanite, Syrian, and later Israelite culture took root. This western edge became a bridge between Egypt and Mesopotamia, and thus became a very important link between two great cultures.

Civilization arose in the Near East. Today oil and politics focus the world's attention to the same area.

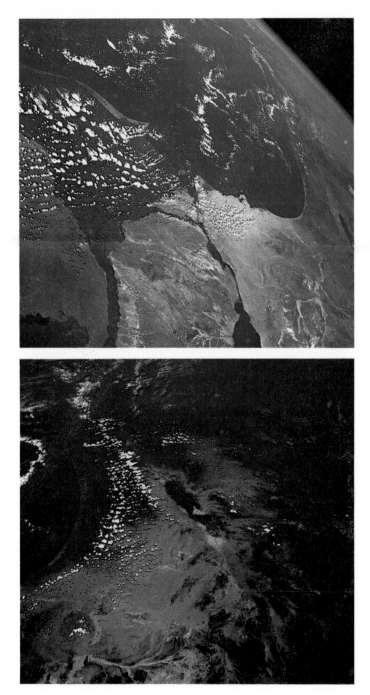

Deserts, mountains, lakes, rivers, and seas made up the physical land where great Bible events took place. The land played an important role in each event, influencing the lifestyle of the people.

Fertile plains were good for farming, rivers for transportation and irrigation, mountains for protection against invaders. Even the deserts provided protection against enemy tribes.

The two photos at the right show the lands of the Bible from outer space. Note the Dead Sea and Sea of Galilee clearly visible in each. Using a Bible atlas, see which Bible-time territories you can find.

Promise Remembered

Noah's first act after leaving the ark was to build an altar and give thank offerings to God. God's first act was to make a commitment to all living beings to never again destroy every living creature. God has set a sign in the skies as a reminder of that ancient promise. It is the rainbow, which accompanies the rains and reminds us and God of His faithfulness.

God placed all the creatures of the earth under man's authority. He was the master of the animal world. At the far right, Noah sees God's rainbow, a promise that a worldwide flood will never come again.

A Promise from God

From Genesis 9

God blessed Noah and his sons and told them, "Be fruitful and multiply and populate the earth again. All animals on earth, the birds of the air, the fish, and everything that crawls on the earth will fear you, for I have placed you over them.

"Every living thing shall be food for you, as I have also given you green plants to eat. But you must not eat meat while the animal's lifeblood remains in it. You must not murder.

"I will require the payment of life for every murder, by his brother I will require that payment. And every animal that kills a man must die.

> "Whoever sheds a man's blood,
> By man shall his blood be shed,
> For man was made
> In the image of God.
> As for you,
> Be fruitful and multiply;
> Repopulate the earth
> And multiply abundantly."

God also said to Noah and his sons, "Listen! I will make a covenant with you and your descendants, with all the living creatures you brought with you on the ark, the birds, cattle, and wild animals. I promise that I will never again destroy all the creatures of the earth with a great flood. I have placed My rainbow in the clouds as a sign of this promise. It shall remain with you as that sign as long as time remains. When the rainbow is in the clouds, I will see it and remember My promise with all living creatures of the earth. This is the sign of My covenant which I have established between Me and all creatures of the earth."

Noah's sons who came from the ark were Shem, Ham, who became the father of Canaan, and Japheth. From these three the whole earth was populated.

After the flood Noah farmed the land and planted a vineyard. One day he drank some of his wine and became drunk, and he lay in his tent naked. Ham, the father of Canaan, looked at his naked father, then went outside to tell his brothers. But Shem and Japheth laid a garment on their shoulders and walked backward, laying the garment over their naked father with their faces turned away so they would not see him.

When Noah awoke, he realized what had happened and

what his youngest son had done. So he spoke this curse:

> "A curse upon Canaan,
> For he will be
> A servant of servants
> To his brothers.
> Blessed be the Lord
> The God of Shem;
> Let Canaan be his servant.
> May God make Japheth great
> To share Shem's wealth
> And dwell in his tents,
> And may Canaan be his servant."

Noah lived three hundred and fifty years after the flood. He was nine hundred and fifty years old when he died.

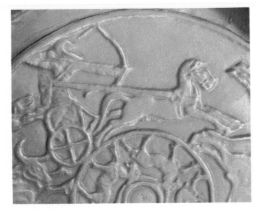

The hunting scene (at the top) comes from the bottom of a fourteenth century B.C. bowl made of gold. It was discovered at Ras Shamra, the site of ancient Ugarit. Both the shepherd's flock and the hunter's catch were essential sources of food for man. God placed only one requirement on man: he must not eat the blood of the animal with its flesh.

BIBLE FOR DAILY LIVING

Bible Truth in Action

The rainbow is a sign of God's promise. To Noah, it was a sign that the earth would never again be destroyed by flood. To us, it is a sign of the same promise. But it is also a sign in the sky that God keeps His promises, for we have had the benefit of thousands of years since Noah saw the first rainbow, and we know that God has kept that promise for all these years. Noah, looking ahead, did not have the proof, only the promise. In one sense, the promise was more glorious to Noah, for he believed it without proof. In another sense, it is more glorious to us, for we have seen it confirmed through all these centuries. Looking ahead or looking back, God's promises are the same, for they are as certain as God Himself.

Words and Meanings

A promise is a pledge from one person to another. It implies: (1) the character, and thus truthfulness, of the one who promises; (2) the assurance that the promised thing will happen because the one who promises will make it happen; and (3) the only failure in the promise will be the failure of the recipient to receive. We can be assured that God's promises will happen because He is truth, unless we fail to receive them in weakness.

The rainbow is still a reminder today of God's promise to Noah.

Noah's Family

Eight people inside the ark provided the only human link between the world before, and the world after, the Great Flood. Through Ham, Shem and Japheth all people on earth today trace their lineage. Each son became the father of many nations.

Japheth was the ancestor of the peoples who lived in Europe and Asia Minor—the Greeks, Thracians and Scythians.

Ham's descendants settled in Egypt, Canaan and Africa. They included the Philistines, Hittites, Amorites and the Jebusites.

From Shem came the ancestors of the Persians, Assyrians, Chaldeans, Lydians and Syrians. The lineage through his son Arpachshad led to Abraham, which led to Jacob and his family, which led to Jesus.

Shem's descendants were also called Semites, and were generally those who spoke Semitic languages, with some exceptions. Semitic languages included Babylonian, Assyrian, Hebrew, Phoenician, Moabite and Arabic. From the Semites came three important world religions—Christianity, Judaism, and Islam.

Scattered

God had told Noah's descendants, "Multiply and fill the earth." But the growing multitude settled together on the future site of Babylon, to build a common city and civilization. God dealt with this disobedience in a unique way. He confused their language. Suddenly the builders could no longer understand each other! Then the separate language groups scattered as God had intended.

The Tower of Babel
From Genesis 11:1-9,27-32

At that time all people of the earth spoke the same language. They began to migrate eastward until a settlement grew up in the land of Shinar, which became known as Babel, or Babylon.

"Let us make a city of bricks and mortar," the people decided. "We will build a great tower in the city which will reach to heaven, bringing us fame and honor. It will unite our people here and prevent us from scattering to other places."

The Lord watched these people build the tower and the city they had planned. "This is not good," the Lord said. "If they band together too much with one language and purpose they may be able to do almost anything. Let Us go down and confuse their language so they will not understand one another."

So the Lord scattered the people across the face of the earth. This ended the construction project at Babel.

The records of the generations of Shem included numerous descendants. One of those descendants was Terah, the father of Abram, Nahor, and Haran. Haran became the father of Lot but died while he was in the land of his birth, at Ur of the Chaldeans, where his father Terah still lived.

Abram married his half-sister Sarai, the daughter of his father Terah but not the daughter of his mother. Nahor married his brother Haran's daughter, whose name was Milcah. (She also had a brother named Iscah.) But Sarai was not able to have children at this time.

In time Terah left Ur of the Chaldeans with his son Abram, his grandson Lot, the orphaned son of Haran, and Abram's

Nebuchadnezzar II built the temple of Ishtar over the site of an earlier tower. Some have suggested that the ruins of his temple mark the site of the biblical tower of Babel.

74

wife Sarai, and they headed for the land of Canaan. But when they reached Haran, they settled there. Terah died at Haran at the age of two hundred and five.

An ancient Jewish tradition identifies the ruined temple at Nimrud as the tower of Babel. Below: workmen build the tower of Babel.

In ancient times the towering temple of Nebo stood over seven stories high.

These Sumerian statuettes were modeled after people who lived over four thousand years ago. They stood in the temple and offered prayers to the gods while their owners were occupied with the concerns of daily life.

BIBLE FOR DAILY LIVING

Bible Truth in Action

The incident at Babel is an example of man's pride and God's response. Literally pride went before a fall in this case, for man's desire to reach toward heaven on his own merits and abilities ended in failure and confusion. It is not wrong to set high goals, only to leave the Lord out of them. It is not wrong to strive for greatness, only to make greatness an opportunity to boast of our own ability instead of the Lord's gracious provision. Pride demands success to satisfy our own ego. Pride claims the credit for success. Humility demands only that God be glorified.

The ziggurat of Ur dominates the site of Abraham's hometown, now in ruins. Above: Abraham leaves Haran with his family.

Personal Enrichment

Look up "pride" in a topical Bible. Search for people who exhibited pride and the circumstances in which they did this. Be sure to include the following: (1) Ahithophel, II Samuel 17:23; (2) Naaman, II Kings 5:11-13; (3) Uzziah, II Chronicles 26:16-19; (4) Haman, Esther 3:5; 5:11,13; 6:6; 7:10; and (5) Nebuchadnezzar, Daniel 4:30-34; 5:20. Also in the topical Bible notice various Scripture references which tell about human pride and the results which come from it.

Personal Checkup

Pride is an unwanted guest in all of our lives. But frequently we discover that pride has come into our lives, invited by us at a time of weakness. Check up on yourself. Ask your motive for wanting your last success. Was it to satisfy your own ego or to make yourself a more effective servant of God? Was it to elevate yourself only, or to bring something better to God, family, and others?

The sledge of Queen Shub-ad (right) was discovered in the royal cemetery at Ur.

The Tower of Babel

After the Flood, a migration of people went to the plain near Shinar and built a large tower. This has most commonly been called the "Tower of Babel," although this name does not appear in the Bible. "Babel" in the native language, Akkadian, meant "the Gate of God." In Hebrew a similar word meant "to mix or confuse."

The tower was a ziggurat, one of several built about this time in that part of the world. It was a temple tower, where people worshiped their gods.

The ziggurat usually resembled a pyramid, was seven stories high, with each story smaller than the one below it, creating

Seven tiers may be seen on the drawing at the left. The small shrine at the top shone with a bright blue color against the sky. This was the "Holy of Holies" for the people who came to worship there.

Some ziggurats had four levels instead of seven. Three stairways met at the top of the first level, becoming one stairway leading to the shrine on the top. The shrine was painted with a bright blue enamel, with some red and black.

The ancient ziggurat (left) looked something like a rainbow. Each of the seven levels was a different color—white, black, red, orange, silver, and gold.

steep tiers or a steplike appearance. It was usually about two to three hundred feet across in each direction at the base. Stairs to the top went up from one level to another. Some towers were cone-shaped with stairs spiralling to the top.

Building material for the ziggurat was mud brick, either the usual mud and straw combination or clay fired at high heat for additional strength. Instead of using mortar, the builders used asphalt to bind the bricks together.

Each of the several levels was painted a different color. The one at the very top was small, probably with one room. It contained a bed and table made of gold. Only the high priestess was allowed to enter this room.

There it was believed the god came to her, and their meeting brought all the people a victorious and fruitful life.

The temple tower itself was built in the center of a large area that contained several smaller temples and towers. Each of these was probably devoted to the worship of one particular god. Very often they were open to the sky so that the gold idols would be brilliant in the sunlight.

The ziggurat was the largest structure in the area. It was easily seen from any part of the city, and served as a reminder to the people of the importance of their god.

The classic type of ziggurat in the northern Near East was the "winding road" variety. There were no staircases in this type. To the far left and below is a bird's-eye view of the temple area surrounding the ziggurat. Some of its many buildings stored grain and taxes; others housed statues and altars.

Faith and Fear

When we meet Abram we meet one of the great figures of history. Moslems, Christians and Jews look on Abram as the father of their faith. Abram did have great faith. He left his homeland, trusting God's promises to him. But even Abram knew fear. When a famine came fear drove Abram from the land God had given him. And fear caused Abram to cower before Pharaoh, Egypt's king, and utter lies.

Pharaoh took Sarai into his harem and showered her "brother" Abram with many gifts. In addition to sheep and camels, Pharaoh gave Abram male and female servants. The reliefs below portray Egyptian slaves in the service of their royal master. Later, Sarai and Abram were sorry that they had not told Pharaoh the truth, that they were husband and wife.

Journey to a New Land
From Genesis 12:1–13:4

After Abram's father died, God commanded him:

> "Go forth from your land,
> From your relatives,
> And from your father's household
> To a land I will show you.
> I will bring forth
> A great nation from you;
> I will bless you,
> And make your name famous.
> You will become a great blessing.
> I will bless those
> Who bless you
> And curse those
> Who curse you.
> In you
> All families of the earth
> Shall be blessed."

At the age of seventy-five Abram left Haran as God commanded, taking Lot with him. He also took his wife Sarai, as well as the servants and possessions he had acquired in Haran. With this caravan, Abram traveled to the land of Canaan.

Abram's caravan went through Canaan to Shechem and camped near the oak of Moreh, a territory which was occupied by the Canaanites at that time. There the Lord appeared to Abram and spoke to him.

"I will give this land to your descendants," the Lord promised Abram. As a memorial to the Lord's visit, Abram built an altar there.

From Shechem Abram moved onward to the hill country east of Bethel and west of Ai. When Abram had set up camp he built another altar to the Lord, and he worshiped the Lord there.

Then Abram moved southward again, passing slowly toward the Negeb. But a severe famine came to the land, so Abram and his family moved to Egypt to live there for a while.

As they approached Egypt, Abram had a talk with Sarai. "I realize that you are a very beautiful woman," Abram told her. "When the Egyptians see you, they may want to kill me and take you alive. Tell them that you are my sister so the Egyptians will show favor to me and spare my life because of you."

When Abram and his caravan arrived in Egypt, the people noticed the beautiful woman with him. Pharaoh's officers noticed her, too and spoke highly of her to the king. Before long Sarai was taken to Pharaoh's palace.

Because of Sarai, Abram was rewarded richly with gifts of flocks, herds, donkeys, male and female slaves, and camels. But the Lord sent great plagues to Pharaoh's household while Sarai lived there.

Pharaoh called for Abram. "Why didn't you tell me that she is your wife?" he demanded. "Why did you say that she is your sister so that I might have married her? Now take your wife and go."

Pharaoh told his men to escort Abram and his people out of the land. So Abram left with his wife, Lot, and all of his possessions, moving back to the Negeb. By this time Abram was very wealthy, for he had livestock and much silver and gold. From the Negeb they moved northward again as far as Bethel, to the place where he had camped before, between Bethel and Ai.

Abram left Egypt with his household and returned to the familiar landscape of the Negeb. In this dry, mountainous region his flocks were free to graze on the scattered patches of wild vegetation.

Colossal figures of Ramses II flank the entrance to the temple of Pharaoh at Abu Simbel.

At right, a statuette of a pharaoh of Egypt at the time of the Patriarchs. Abram and Sarai met pharaohs such as this and the one above.

Abram went to Egypt because the famine had not reached the land of the Nile. At left, a banquet scene from an Egyptian funeral stele.

Vast stretches of the Negeb (below) remain uninhabited. The terrain has changed little since the days of Abram.

BIBLE FOR DAILY LIVING

Bible Quiz

Facts are the framework for Bible understanding. A quiz such as this helps you recall the facts you have learned during the past three readings:

1. The rainbow was God's promise that He would never again
   a. send a flood   b. destroy all creatures of the earth by flood
2. Noah's son Ham became the father of
   a. Israel   b. Canaan
3. After the flood, Noah lived for how many years?
   a. 120   b. 350   c. 600
4. Babel, in the land of Shinar, became known as
   a. Babylon   b. Israel   c. Egypt
5. Abram's (Abraham's) hometown was
   a. Babylon   b. Ur   c. Jerusalem
6. Abram's father was
   a. Nahor   b. Terah   c. Haran
7. When Abram migrated from Haran to Canaan, he was how old?
   a. 30   b. 50   c. 75
8. Abram's wife Sarai was also his
   a. cousin   b. half sister   c. niece
9. Abram migrated from Canaan to Egypt because
   a. he went in search of gold   b. there was a famine in Canaan

Answers: 1b, 2b, 3b, 4a, 5b, 6b, 7c, 8b, 9b

The Bible comes alive

Ur—Abraham's Hometown

Throughout his childhood and youth, Abraham lived in or near the city of Ur. It was probably at least a thousand years old at that time, and was an important center of Mesopotamia, the region around and between the Tigris and Euphrates Rivers.

In its early years, including the time of Abraham, Mesopotamia's southern section was called Sumer, and was inhabited by the Sumerians, the dominant people of Mesopotamia. Later Babylon dominated Mesopotamia, and still later, Assyria. After Assyria fell, the land was ruled by the Persians, then Greeks, then Romans.

Ur was one of the most important cities of Sumer. It was built on the banks of the Euphrates River and was surrounded by a complicated system of man-made canals. An oval wall protected it from attack. Fields beyond the wall supplied the city with food.

Members of the royal family of Ur were buried with their possessions and personal attendants. Above is a reconstruction of the scene in the death pit.

Ladies-in-waiting were buried in their finery. At left, a wreath of gold leaves and a choker necklace recovered from a tomb.

The headdress of Queen Shub-ad (upper right) was recovered from the death pit of Ur. The skull of the Sumerian queen helped archaeologists to recreate her features in wax.

With painstaking care archaeologists restored the golden lyre (above, right) which was crushed by the weight of the earth.

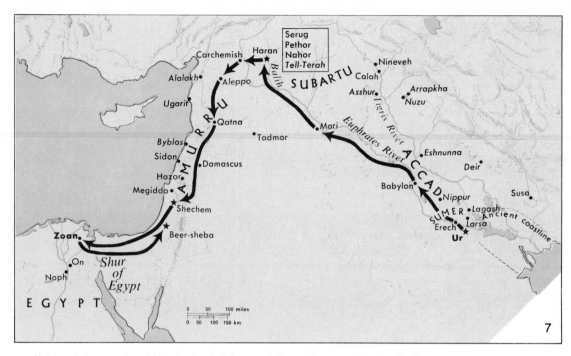

Abraham's journey from Ur to the land of Canaan followed the arc of the Fertile Crescent.

The most striking building in Ur was a ziggurat, a great tiered tower similar to the Tower of Babel, but three stories instead of seven. This ziggurat, originally about seventy feet high, was dedicated to Nanna, the moon god of Ur. Nanna was considered the true "owner" and ruler of the city.

The human king was Nanna's representative before the people. He was also responsible for maintaining order and providing military protection. Each morning the king held court to hear the grievances of the people.

By modern standards the average person in Ur lived poorly. A house was usually a one-story mud-brick building without windows. Crowded among its neighboring houses, it faced a narrow, muddy street without sewers or pavement.

Streets in the public sector of the city were broad and well-traveled. The public marketplace or bazaar was a bustling center of activity. The Sumerians gathered there for trade and to exchange news.

Farmers brought their produce in from the fields and offered a great variety of food. Onions, apples, barley and fish were displayed side by side with exotic wares imported from India or what is now Iran, brought there by traveling merchants.

Although minor transactions were handled without receipts, important business deals were recorded by professional scribes on clay tablets.

The aristocracy of Ur lived comfortably, attended by slaves and surrounded with luxurious works of Sumerian art. These works of art have been discovered in the tombs of nobles and may be seen today.

The Sumerians developed an advanced system of writing with which they recorded their growth and history. Much of what is known today about Abraham's neighbors comes from their own written records unearthed from the ruins of ancient Ur.

Leisure time was the privilege of the upper class in ancient Ur. Wealthy Sumerians enjoyed whiling away the time with games. These gaming boards were discovered in the royal tombs at Ur. Their geometric patterns recall a modern checkerboard although the rules of the game differed from our own version of checkers.

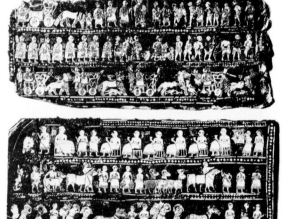

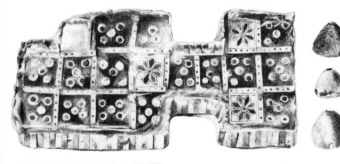

Scenes from daily life in ancient Sumeria are preserved on the Standard of Ur. Inlaid with shell and lapis lazuli, these two panels contain a wealth of information about Abraham's neighbors. The upper panel portrays the Sumerians at war while the lower panel depicts a procession on its way to court.

Lot's Choice

Many chapters of Genesis are filled with stories of men and women like us. We read of their hopes and fears, their choices and the result of those choices. Lot was a nephew of Abram. Both men gained great wealth in herds of animals. When the time came for them to separate, Abram gave Lot first choice of the land. Would Lot choose the hill country, or the rich valley land near the city of Sodom? And what events would flow from his decision?

Abram and Lot knew that the time had come
to divide their households. The land could
not support the herds of both. Abram gave
his nephew the first choice, offering
to take whichever portion Lot declined.

The War of Nine Kings
From Genesis 13:5–14:24

Like Abram, Lot was becoming a wealthy man with sheep, cattle, and servants. But the land could not support both men with all their possessions while they lived together. Also, the Canaanites and Perizzites were still living in the land.

Before long the herdsmen of Lot and Abram began to quarrel. "Let's not quarrel," Abram told Lot. "Our herdsmen must not quarrel either, for we are the same family. Choose the land you want and I will take what remains. If you want that part over there, I'll take this part. If you want this part, I'll take that part over there."

Lot studied the land carefully and noticed especially the well-watered, fertile plains of the Jordan River. Before the Lord destroyed Sodom and Gomorrah, this land was like the garden of Eden or the land around Zoar in Egypt.

So Lot chose the Jordan Valley and the land to the east for himself. Lot and Abram separated, and Lot moved to the new land with his flocks and servants. While Abram remained in Canaan, Lot settled among the cities of the plain, setting up camp near the city of Sodom. But the men of Sodom were wicked and sinned greatly against the Lord.

After Lot had moved away, the Lord spoke to Abram. "Look in every direction, north, east, south, west, as far as you can see. I will give all the land you can see to your descendants forever. Your descendants will be as numerous as the dust of the earth. If anyone can count the dust of the earth, then he can also count your descendants. Now walk throughout this land, for it will be your heritage."

So Abram moved his tent and settled by the oaks of Mamre, near Hebron. There he built an altar to the Lord.

In those days war came to the land when five kings rebelled against King Chedorlaomer of Elam. The five who rebelled were Bera king of Sodom, Birsha king of Gomorrah, Shinab king of Admah, Shemeber king of Zeboiim, and the king of Bela, which was later called Zoar.

These five kings had been subject to Chedorlaomer for twelve years; but in the thirteenth year they rallied their armies in Siddim Valley, the valley by the Salt Sea. The next year Chedorlaomer swept across the land with his allies, Amraphel king of Shinar, Arioch king of Ellasar, and Tidal king of nations. First they conquered the Rephaim in Ashteroth-karnaim, the Zuzim at Ham, the Emim in the plain of

Kiriathaim, and the Horites in Mount Seir, as far as El-paran near the desert.

From there the conquerors turned to Enmishpat, which is Kadesh, and conquered all the land of the Amalekites as well as the Amorites who lived in Hazazon-tamar. Then the five kings of Sodom, Gomorrah, Admah, Zeboiim, and Bela attacked Chedorlaomer and his allies in the Siddim Valley. But the armies of the five kings were defeated; and as they retreated some of the men fell into the asphalt pits which were scattered throughout the valley. The survivors fled to the mountains.

Chedorlaomer and his troops took all the wealth and food of Sodom and Gomorrah and headed toward home, taking Abram's nephew Lot and all his possessions also. But one man escaped and reported these events to Abram, who was camping among the oaks of Mamre the Amorite, the brother of Eshcol and Aner, allies of Abram.

Abram immediately rallied the three hundred and eighteen men of his household and pursued Chedorlaomer's forces as far as Dan. When night came he attacked, chasing the army as far as Hobah, north of Damascus. Abram recaptured all the goods and people Chedorlaomer had taken including Lot and his possessions and the women and other captives.

As Abram returned from his victory over Chedorlaomer and the other kings, the king of Sodom went out to meet him at the

At left are the mountains of Moab beyond the eastern shore of the Dead Sea.

Salt flats (below) form at the shallow southern end of the Dead Sea.

Archaeologists believe that the cities of the plain lay in the area now flooded by the southern portion of the Dead Sea.

Like an abstract sculpture, a half- submerged piece of driftwood lies close to the shore of the Dead Sea.

Dan lies in the far north of Palestine, at the base of Mount Hermon. Abram and his allies pursued Chedorlaomer's army to this region and attacked the Elamites by night.

Valley of Shaveh, the King's Valley. Melchizedek, the king of Salem (Jerusalem) and priest of the Most High God, met Abram there, too, bringing him food and wine.

Melchizedek blessed Abram, saying,

"May the blessings of the Most High God,
Maker of heaven and earth,
Be upon you Abram,
And blessed be the Most High God,
Who has delivered your enemies
Into your hands."

And Abram gave Melchizedek a tenth of all the goods he had captured in battle.

"Keep all of the goods for yourself," the king of Sodom told Abram. "Give me only my people who were captured from my city."

"No, I have sworn to the Lord God Most High, Maker of heaven and earth, that I would not take a thread or sandal-thong or anything that is yours," Abram answered. "For if I do you might say that you have made Abram rich. I will take only what my young men have eaten and the portion of the goods to which my allies, Aner, Eshcol, and Mamre are entitled. Give each of them their rightful share."

BIBLE FOR DAILY LIVING

Bible Truth in Action

Two incidents are recorded in this reading. One tells how most ancient people solved their disagreements. "War came to the land when five kings rebelled." The other tells how Abram solved the disagreement between him and his nephew Lot. "Choose the land you want and I will take what remains." Abram's method was not typical of ancients or moderns. Most people, like the five kings, rebel and start war or fighting. The reason is typical also—to put self first and to get, not give. Abram's method was to give, not get, to avoid fighting and war by putting the other person first. His son Isaac would exhibit the same peacemaking quality many years later when the Philistines would take his wells. Jesus, centuries later, said that peacemakers are blessed, or happy. Abram, the peacemaker, was truly blessed.

Personal Checkup

Think back to the last time you had a disagreement with someone. What was at stake? Was it ego, or personal pride? Did you fight for it, or seek to put the other person first?

Prayer Pointers

Lord, like my neighbors, I strive often to put myself above others, and sometimes above Your desires. Help me think of divine priorities—You first, others second, self third.

With his victory, Abram gathered great spoils, wealth which a victorious army captured from the enemy.

The Battle of the Kings

Chedorlaomer, Amraphel and Shemeber, names of ancient kings, sound strange to modern ears. Who were these long-ago rulers and where did they reign?

In the days of Abraham, the land of Canaan was divided among many petty kings. Each city had its own king and worshiped its own gods. Although two cities might be within sight of one another, they remained individual kingdoms with separate armies.

In the region of the Dead Sea, a cluster of these Canaanite city-states were ruled by five separate kings: Berea, king of Sodom; Birsha, king of Gomorrah; Shinab, king of Admah; Shemeber, king of Zeboiim; and the unnamed king of Zoar (Bela).

For twelve years they had paid tribute to Chedorlaomer, king of Elam, but their restlessness finally broke out into revolt. Each one by himself did not have the strength to rebel against Chedorlaomer, but the five together formed a powerful army, and they joined forces against their Mesopotamian overlord.

When the cities of the plain withheld their tribute from Chedorlaomer, the Elamite king called his four allies to war. With the support of Arioch, king of Ellasar; Tidal, king of Goiim and Amraphel, king of Shinar, Chedorlaomer marched west and south, following the arc of the fertile crescent. On the Jordan plain he met the five rebel kings.

Although the alliance of Canaanite kings outnumbered the supporters of Chedorlaomer, the rebel army could not match the skill of the Mesopotamian forces. Chedorlaomer defeated the Canaanite kings thoroughly, scattering their armies and destroying them. He looted their cities, plundering them of riches and carrying off their inhabitants as slaves.

Lot, Abraham's nephew, was among the captives destined for slavery in Mesopotamia. The manner in which Abraham traveled to the north and attacked the forces at night shows his wisdom and power as a warrior. Armies did not usually try to fight at night, so the enemy was totally surprised and thrown into panic.

But the manner in which Abraham shared a tithe of the booty with Melchizedek showed his devotion to God and His priest. Abraham also refused to keep the other nine-tenths of the booty, considering his reputation more important than wealth.

The silent shores of the Dead Sea witnessed the battle of the kings. Chedorlaomer and his allies fought the rebel kings in the surrounding valley.

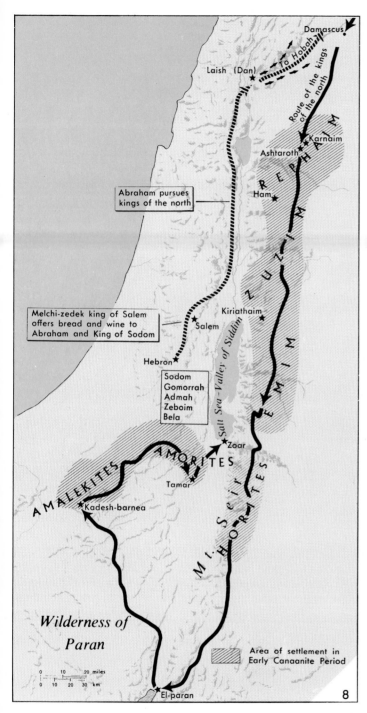

Abraham pursues kings of the north

Melchi-zedek king of Salem offers bread and wine to Abraham and King of Sodom

Sodom
Gomorrah
Admah
Zeboim
Bela

Salt Sea-Valley of Siddim

Damascus

Laish (Dan)

To Hobah

Route of the kings of the north

REPHAIM

Karnaim

Ashtaroth

Ham

ZUZIM

Kiriathaim

EMIM

Salem

Hebron

Zoar

Tamar

Mt. Seir HORITES

AMALEKITES

AMORITES

Kadesh-barnea

Wilderness of Paran

Area of settlement in Early Canaanite Period

0   10   20 miles
0   10   20   30   km

El-paran

8

Following the major north-south trade route, the northern kings descended on the rebel alliance.

At top is the Dead Sea as it appears from space. The ruins of Sodom and Gomorrah are believed to lie beneath its waters at the southern end.

The Dead Sea Valley was an important population center in Abraham's day. Irrigation made the area green and pleasant. Today this sparsely peopled region has returned to the desert (above).

Promise Renewed

When God first spoke to Abram He promised to make him a great nation. Years passed. Abram and his wife, Sarah, remained childless. Then God spoke again. "Count the stars," He said. "Your descendants will be as numerous." In spite of his advanced age, Abram believed the promise. Then, to show how sure the promise was, God made an unbreakable covenant: a contract known in Abram's time as a covenant of blood.

A Promised Son

From Genesis 15–16

After the war of the kings had ended, the Lord spoke to Abram in a vision. "Do not be afraid Abram, for I am your Shield," the Lord said. "I will reward you richly with great blessings."

"But Lord, I have no son," Abram cried out. "How can I enjoy Your blessings without a son to be my heir, knowing that Eliezer of Damascus will inherit all that You give me? Since You have given me no child, a slave will inherit all I have."

"Eliezer will not be your heir," the Lord answered. "Your own son will be your heir."

The Lord brought Abram outside under the great canopy of the sky. "Look up into the heavens and count the stars, if you can," the Lord said. "Your descendants will be as many as the stars of the sky tonight."

Abram believed the Lord, and the Lord accepted him as righteous because he believed. Then the Lord told him, "I am the Lord Who brought you from Ur of the Chaldeans to give you this land forever as a possession."

"But how can I know for sure that this will be mine?" Abram asked.

"Bring Me a three-year-old heifer, a three-year-old female goat, a three-year-old ram, a turtle-dove, and a young pigeon," the Lord told Abram.

Like Abram, the Bedouin of the Middle East today live in tents. They follow their herds from place to place, continually in search of pasture.

The night sky glittered with more stars than Abram could possibly count! Their number was so great that God's promise stretched beyond the limits of his imagination.

Abram brought all of the animals, cut them in half, and laid the halves opposite each other. But he did not cut the birds in half. When birds of prey swooped down to devour these sacrifices, Abram drove them away.

As the sun was setting a deep sleep came upon Abram and an overwhelming feeling of darkness swept over him. Then the Lord spoke again to Abram.

"Your descendants will be slaves in a foreign land for four hundred years," the Lord told him. "They will work for those who oppress them but I will punish the nation they serve and later they will go free with great wealth. But you will die in peace and be buried at a ripe old age. Your descendants will return here in four generations, for the wickedness of the Amorites will come to full fruit at that time."

When the sun had set and darkness had come over the land, Abram saw a smoking fire pot and a flaming torch passing among the pieces of meat. Then the Lord made a covenant with Abram. "To your descendants I give this land from the River of Egypt to the Great River, the Euphrates, along with the peoples therein—the Kenite, the Kenizzite, the Kadmonite, the Hittite, the Perizzite, the Rephaim, the Amorite, the Canaanite, the Girgashite and the Jebusite."

Sarai was still childless at this time so she decided to give her Egyptian maid Hagar to Abram as a second wife, to bear children for her.

Donkeys drink from the water of a desert spring which emerges in the middle of the Negeb, the land where Abraham spent much of his life.

"The Lord has not given me children," Sarai told Abram. "Try to have children through Hagar and her children will also be my children."

Abram listened to Sarai's idea and agreed to take Hagar as a second wife. At this time Abram had been in the land for ten years. As soon as Hagar knew that she would have a child, she began to look upon Sarai with contempt.

"I hope you suffer as I have," Sarai told Abram. "I put my maid into your arms, and as soon as she knew that she would have a child, she began to look upon me with contempt."

"But your maid is in your own power," Abram argued. "Do whatever you want to her."

Then Sarai treated Hagar so harshly that she ran away. While Hagar sat by a spring of water in the wilderness an angel appeared to her. "Where have you come from Hagar?" the angel asked, "and where are you going?"

"I am running away from Sarai, my mistress," Hagar answered the angel.

"Go home to Sarai and submit to her," the angel commanded. "I will give you so many descendants that you will not be able to count them. You will have a son whom you will name Ishmael, for the Lord has noticed your affliction. Ishmael will be like a wild donkey, against everyone and everyone against him, although he will continue to live near his relatives."

Hagar realized that this was the Lord speaking to her so she called Him "The Seeing God." For she said, "Haven't I seen God yet I am still alive?" Then Hagar named the spring "Well of the Living One Who Sees Me." This well was located between Kadesh and Bered.

In time Hagar presented a son to Abram and Abram named him Ishmael. Abram was eighty-six when Ishmael was born.

BIBLE FOR DAILY LIVING

People Profiles

Look up "Abraham" in a Bible dictionary. List the qualities you find in the dictionary which tell about Abraham. Look up Scripture references given so that you may become acquainted with the person and his profile. Ask the following questions concerning Abraham (Abram): (1) Was he obedient to God or disobedient? (2) Was he a proud man or humble? (3) Was he a man of God or a man of the world? (4) Did Abraham believe everything that God said or did he doubt?

Something to Think About

The term "righteous" often suggests godly conduct. A man or woman is righteous if he or she does what pleases God. But an interesting phrase appears in today's reading, "Abram believed the Lord, and the Lord accepted him as righteous because he believed." Thus Abram's righteous conduct was belief. This reminds us of the New Testament, where righteousness is not our own good works, but belief in the Lord and His plan of redemption.

Prayer Pointers

Lord, sometimes it is easier to doubt than to believe in Your Word. Help me to believe. When Your promises seem impossible, as they must have seemed to Abram, help me remember that with You nothing is impossible, that the Lord Who made the world and all that is in it is capable of managing the world's affairs as He chooses.

By a desert spring Hagar received God's promise that she would be the mother of a great people.

God chose Abraham's family
as the channel through
which He would bring
salvation to all mankind.
"In you shall all the
nations of the earth be
blessed," He told Abraham.
That promise was fulfilled
in the death of Jesus
Christ for the sins of the
world. His blood sealed
the covenant between God
and man.

Covenants

In Bible times, a covenant was a solemn agreement between two people. Both worked out the terms of their agreement and swore in the presence of God to honor all of the promises made in the covenant. A curse, included in the covenant, pronounced punishment or death if either party failed to uphold his half of the agreement. The word covenant is still used today by lawyers to describe certain kinds of contracts.

Just as two businessmen shake hands after closing an important deal, the men of ancient times concluded their covenant with a special ceremony. They offered a sacrifice to God and shared the flesh of the sacrificial victim in a ritual meal. This solemn occasion marked the moment when the covenant went into effect.

But not every covenant made in Bible times was an agreement between individuals. Nations covenanted together to form political alliances or to establish peace among themselves. These treaties helped maintain a fragile balance of power in the Bible world.

If one nation broke its covenant with another, the delicate balance was upset and armies began preparing for war. When the fighting was over and one nation had emerged as the victor over the other, a new covenant was established between them. The agreement, originally between equals, was now a treaty imposed by the conqueror on the conquered.

These one-sided covenants placed all the obligations on the weaker party. But there are other examples of contracts in which the stronger member was responsible for fulfilling all the covenant promises. A rich man's will was a one-sided covenant in which he promised to distribute his wealth among his poor relatives. His heirs were not bound by the covenant to meet any requirements; they could accept or reject the rich man's offer.

God used covenants also. The Old Testament was His covenant with Israel, first made with Abraham and extended to later generations. The Lord promised to be their God and to give them the land of Canaan. In return they were to worship Him and obey His law, with failure punishable by death.

But God understood peoples' weaknesses. They were not capable of meeting every requirement of His law. So He established a system of sacrifices by which they could atone for their sins. The sacrificial lamb suffered death in their place and preserved the covenant between God and His people.

The Israelites turned away from God and worshiped foreign deities. They set up idols in the temple and neglected to offer sacrifices to God. They broke the old covenant by their behavior. But the Lord did not abandon men. Instead, He made a new covenant that extended to all mankind.

In the New Testament, God took upon Himself a share of man's covenant responsibilities. He provided His own Son as the sacrificial Lamb to bear the curse of death. Christ's blood has atoned for mankind's sins as one great sacrifice. Animal victims are no longer to be offered for sin. Under the new covenant people everywhere are like the rich man's heirs. God has met all the covenant conditions and people have only to decide whether to accept or reject His offer.

Past Hope?

Years after God's promise in the stars, Abram and Sarah still had no child. They were long past the age of childbearing: there seemed to be no hope. Then God spoke again. God changed the name Abram (which meant "Father") to Abraham (which meant "Father of a Multitude"). God, who created a universe from nothing, would bring miracle life from the aging pair. Isaac, their son, is a reminder that with God we are never past hope.

God's Covenant with Abraham
From Genesis 17

The Lord appeared once more to Abram when he was ninety-nine years old. "I am the Almighty God," the Lord told Abram. "Walk with Me and please Me. I will make My covenant with you and will multiply you greatly."

Abram knelt with his face to the ground as God continued to speak to him. "My covenant is with you, and I will make you the father of many nations. No longer will you be called Abram, but your new name will be Abraham, which means "Father of Nations," for I will make you the father of many descendants throughout numerous lands, and some will be kings. My covenant will be with you and your descendants for many generations to come, a covenant to be your God and the God of your descendants. I will give the land of Canaan to you and them forever, and I will be their God.

"But you and your descendants must keep My covenant. You must be circumcised as a sign between Me and you. Every boy must be circumcised eight days after he is born, whether he is a member of your family, or a servant boy, or a slave boy bought with money. Thus My covenant will leave its mark on your flesh as an everlasting sign. Any male who refuses to be circumcised refuses My covenant, and he shall be cut off from his people."

Then the Lord spoke to Abraham concerning Sarai. "Her name shall be called Sarah from this time on" He commanded. "I will bless her and give you a son through her. She will become a mother of nations and kings shall come forth from her."

Abraham knelt before the Lord to worship, but he laughed when he heard God's promise. "How can I have a son when I am a hundred years old?" he thought. "And how can Sarah have a child when she is ninety?"

Then Abraham spoke aloud to the Lord. "Oh, God, bless Ishmael!" he cried out, assuming that God was speaking of Ishmael.

"But Sarah will have a son," God answered. "You will name him Isaac, and I will make My covenant forever with him and his descendants. I have also heard your prayer for Ishmael and will bless him and give him many descendants. He will be the father of twelve princes and of a great nation. But my covenant will be with Isaac, who will be born to you and Sarah about this time next year."

When the Lord finished speaking, He left Abraham alone. That very day Abraham circumcised all the males of his household, including Ishmael and the servants born in his household and the slaves he had bought, just as the Lord had commanded.

Abraham was ninety-nine years old when he was circumcised, and his son Ishmael was thirteen. That very same day both Abraham and Ishmael were circumcised, as well as all the men of Abraham's household, including all of Abraham's servants and slaves.

BIBLE FOR DAILY LIVING

Bible Quiz
Test your Bible memory with the following questions:
1. When Abram and Lot separated, Lot settled near the city of
   a. Sodom   b. Canaan   c. Jerusalem
2. Abram settled by the oaks of Mamre, which were near
   a. Sodom   b. Canaan   c. Hebron
3. The king of Sodom, along with four other kings in the area, rebelled against
   a. Abram   b. Chedorlaomer
4. The king of Sodom and his allies were
   a. victorious   b. defeated
5. In this battle, Abram's nephew Lot was
   a. captured by Chedorlaomer   b. killed
6. When Abram defeated Chedorlaomer, he gave a tenth of the spoils to
   a. Lot   b. the king of Sodom   c. Melchizedek, king of Jerusalem
7. Until Abram had a son, his heir was
   a. Eliezer of Damascus   b. Lot
8. Sarai gave her maid to Abram as a wife. Her name was
   a. Rachel   b. Rebekah   c. Hagar
9. The child which Abram and Hagar had was named
   a. Ishmael   b. Isaac
10. Isaac was named by God before he was born.   T   F
11. Abram's name was changed to
    a. Israel   b. Ishmael   c. Abraham
12. The name Abraham meant
    a. Covenant   b. Father of Nations   c. Circumcised

Answers: 1a, 2c, 3b, 4b, 5a, 6c, 7a, 8c, 9a, 10T, 11c, 12b

Many ancient rulers took pride in their building accomplishments. Temples, walls, and towers were lasting monuments to their leadership. At right, a Sumerian king is portrayed as a mortar bearer.

Abraham's Sumerian Roots

The bleak Mesopotamian plain seems an unlikely birthplace for human civilization, yet it was here that the ancient Sumerians flourished almost five thousand years ago. They were attracted to the "Land between the Rivers," the Tigris and Euphrates River Valleys, by the abundance of life-giving water and the rich soil along the banks of the rivers.

Sumer was not a country with a single ruler. It was a confederation of individual cities that shared a common culture. Each city had its own king and its own gods.

During the time of Abraham, Sumerian political power was declining. Many years of war between the cities had weakened their defenses and opened the way for attack by outsiders.

But in spite of its fading military strength, Sumerian civilization remained one of the most advanced cultures in the ancient world. The men of Sumer were expert and skilled craftsmen. They knew how to combine copper and tin to make bronze, from which they could forge stronger tools. They also understood how to build self-supporting arches, which some people believe made modern architecture possible.

Early in their history the Sumerians invented a practical system of writing with which to record their business transactions. Many clay tablets have been found impressed with the symbols of ancient trade deals. Eventually writing became the foundation for a wide variety of literature. The Sumerians left behind written law codes, medical textbooks and mythological stories. Much has been learned about the world in which Abraham lived from these ancient Sumerian "books."

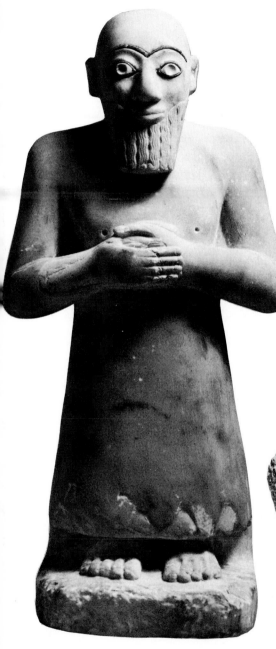

Gudea (below) was the pious prince of Lagash. He preserved peace in his city during an age of political upheaval. The Gutians, fierce invaders from the north, had overrun Sumeria and captured control of many of her cities. Gudea ruled about the time Abraham lived.

The statuette of a Sumerian worshiper provides us with a glimpse into the past. This bearded figurine stood in the temple of a Sumerian god and begged the deities to grant long life and good fortune to its owner.

Dangerous Prayer?

God announced to Abraham His intention to destroy the city of Sodom for its wickedness. Fearfully Abraham begged God not to act if even a righteous few could be found there. Would God be angry with Abraham for daring to question the rightness of His plan?

Abraham Bargains for Sodom
From Genesis 18

One hot day as Abraham sat by the door of his tent among the oaks at Mamre, he noticed three strangers approaching. Abraham immediately ran out to meet them, bowing to the ground.

"Please don't pass by my tent," said Abraham. "I will bring some water to wash your feet and you can rest under the tree. I'll bring something to eat so you can refresh yourselves before going on your way."

"All right, please do as you have said," the men answered.

Abraham ran back to the tent to find Sarah. "Take three

Bedouin life exists in a world without time. Thousands of years have brought little change to their way of life, including the tents which are their homes.

measures of flour, knead it, and quickly make some cakes of bread."

Then Abraham ran out to his herd of animals, found a calf with good, tender meat and gave it to his servant to prepare. When the calf was ready, Abraham took curds and milk and the meat and set it before the strangers. While they ate, he stood nearby under the tree.

"Where is your wife Sarah?" the men asked.

"In the tent," Abraham answered.

Then the Lord, speaking as one of the men, said to Abraham, "This time next year I will return. When I do, your wife Sarah will have had a son."

Sarah was listening by the door of the tent behind Him as

He spoke. When she heard what the Lord said, she laughed, for she and Abraham were much too old to have a child.

"How can I have a baby now when I and my husband are both so old?" Sarah scoffed.

But the Lord spoke to Abraham about this. "Why did Sarah laugh? And why did she doubt that she can have a child when she is so old?" the Lord asked. "Is anything too difficult for the Lord to do? I will return next year and Sarah will have a son by that time."

Sarah was afraid now and denied that she had laughed. "I didn't laugh," she argued.

"But you did!" the Lord answered.

Then the men arose to leave, heading toward Sodom. Abraham went with them for some distance, which was a courtesy to guests.

"Should I hide what I am about to do from Abraham?" the Lord wondered. "Some day his people will become a mighty nation and through them he will cause the nations of the world to be blessed. And since I have chosen him and his family to keep the way of the Lord and fulfil what I have promised, should I keep from him this secret?"

So the Lord told Abraham about His plans. "The wickedness of Sodom and Gomorrah cries out to Me, and their sin is very great," the Lord said. "I will go there to see if these things are true."

From inside the tent Sarah overheard the Lord's prophecy. She laughed at the idea that she would have a child in her old age.

117

The two men went on toward Sodom while the Lord remained with Abraham for a while. Then Abraham began to ask the Lord about His coming judgment.

"Will you destroy the righteous with the wicked?" he asked. "What if there are fifty righteous people in the city? Will you destroy the city? Will you not spare it for their sake? Surely you would not destroy the righteous with the wicked for that would be treating the righteous and wicked alike. I am sure that the Judge of all the Earth will be just."

The Lord answered, "If I find fifty righteous people in Sodom, I will spare the whole city because of them."

"Since I have asked this question, let me continue," Abraham said. "I know that I am only dust and ashes, but suppose there are only forty-five righteous people in Sodom?"

Then the Lord said, "I will not destroy the city if there are forty-five righteous people there."

Again Abraham spoke to the Lord. "But suppose there are only forty?"

"I will spare the city for forty righteous people," the Lord replied.

"Please don't be angry but let me ask again. What if there are only thirty righteous people there?"

"I will not destroy the city for thirty people," the Lord answered.

"Let me ask once again. Suppose there are only twenty?" Abraham said.

"Then I will spare the city for the sake of the twenty," the Lord responded.

At last Abraham said, "Oh, Lord, please don't be angry. I will ask only once more. What if you find only ten righteous people?"

And God answered, "For the sake of the ten, I will not destroy the city."

As soon as He had finished speaking with Abraham, the Lord went on His way. And Abraham returned home.

A stone marker points the way to ancient Mamre. Its Arabic name, Ramat el-Khalil, means "the high place of the friend of God."

BIBLE FOR DAILY LIVING

Bible Truth in Action

There is a saying about entertaining angels unawares. Abraham discovered the truth about this saying, for the Lord visited his tent near Mamre in human form. The Lord's visit was twofold—to remind Abraham and Sarah of the coming birth of their promised son, and to tell Abraham of the Lord's plans to destroy Sodom and Gomorrah. Thus the Lord brought news of joy and anticipation along with news of judgment and destruction. In our homes we have the Bible, God's Word, filled with news of both joy and judgment. Both are necessary. Without the promise of joy to come, life would be too stern and futile. But without warnings of coming judgment, life would be preoccupied with today's pleasures. Like angels unawares, the Bible resides as a permanent guest in our homes, bringing these two messages for those who will listen.

Words and Meanings

''Justice'' and ''judgment'' may at first sound harsh and uninviting. But how would it be to live in a world without justice or judgment, without adequate punishment for evil or a deterrent for crime? Justice speaks of a proper punishment or reward for conduct. A person gets what he deserves. Justice is necessary to restrain evil, and to promote good. But in the New Testament, God offers another alternative—mercy. For those who truly repent of evil and seek Him, He grants forgiveness and mercy. In this new concept, a person does not get what he deserves. Instead, he is offered new life, new hope, new forgiveness, and new opportunity without a lasting judgment.

Prayer Pointers

Lord, remind me daily of Your justice and mercy. Help me remember that unforgiven sin demands justice. Help me remember also that through Your Son I may have mercy, forgiveness for my sins and new hope for tomorrow.

Beneath the ruins of ancient Jewish and Christian shrines at Mamre, archaeologists have discovered pottery dating back to the time of Abraham.

This Galilean woman makes cakes of bread by the same method used in Bible times.

Green fields and vineyards grow in the area near Mamre, where Abraham once pitched his tent (left).

The Bible comes alive

Hospitality

In Old Testament times hospitality was an important duty. When a guest arrived he was treated as if he were the master of the house even though his host may never have met him before. When he received his guest the host always kept in mind that someday he too might be a traveler in need of food and shelter. He also thought that the stranger might be a messenger from God.

Sharing a meal created a special bond between the host and his guest. Although meat was costly and rarely eaten, a host would willingly kill a member of his flocks to provide a meal for his guest. As a sign of special respect the master of the house actually served the food himself and stood by while his guests ate.

At this time it was customary to eat only two meals a day. The noon meal was a light lunch of bread, fruit and olives. The major meal was served at the end of the working day, shortly before sunset. Everyone sat on mats spread over the ground. A common bowl was set in the center, often on a low table. Forks and knives were unknown; everyone dipped his bread in the bowl and ate it with his fingers. As a sign of respect, the host dipped his bread into the bowl and offered it to the guest.

Other customs surrounded the meal as well. Before sitting down to eat, the host provided water so that the guests could wash the dust of the road from their feet. He also or-

dered a servant to anoint them with oil, the Bible-time substitute for soap. Sometimes he even provided his guests with special festive garments of white.

Custom dictated that a guest could stay in his host's home for three days. During that time he was under the protection of his host. At the end of those three days he was expected to leave and continue his journey even though good manners forced the host to urge him to stay longer.

But even after the traveler set out again his host's duties were not complete. The host was expected to accompany him for a short distance as an escort of honor sending him on his way.

Among the Bedouin tribes in modern Bible lands, many ancient customs of hospitality are still observed with great care.

A good host in Bible times always kept a supply of wine on hand for unexpected guests. Before offering the traveler a cup, he filtered out the dregs by pouring the wine from one jug into another. The wine jugs pictured here date back to the time of Abraham.

Judgment and Mercy

The wickedness of Sodom is clearly portrayed in the Bible. God's terrible judgment of fiery destruction was well deserved. But even in His anger, God remembered mercy. Lot and his family were led out of the city to safety.

The Destruction of Sodom
From Genesis 19

Lot was sitting by the gate of Sodom that evening when the two angels arrived from Abraham's tent. As soon as he saw them he stood up to greet them, bowing with his face to the ground.

"Please come to my house tonight," Lot said. "You may spend the night with me, then rise up as early as you wish and be on your way."

"No, we will spend the night in the street," they answered.

But Lot insisted, so they went with him to his house where he prepared a feast for them with baked, unleavened bread. The angels ate the dinner, but before they lay down to sleep, the men of Sodom surrounded the house. There were young men and old men, from every part of the city.

The Sodomites called out to Lot: "Where are those men who came to your house tonight? Bring them out so we can molest them."

Lot stepped outside the house, closing the door behind him. "Please, my brothers, don't do such a wicked thing," he

High, barren mountains border the Dead Sea on the east and the west.

124

Intent on evil, the men of Sodom surrounded Lot's house. When Lot refused to surrender his guests to the mob, they threatened to break down his doors.

Archaeologists believe that the ancient cities of Sodom and Gomorrah lie beneath the shallow waters at the southern end of the Dead Sea.

said to the villagers. "You may even have my two virgin daughters, but don't bother these men, for they are my guests."

"Stand aside!" the men of Sodom ordered. They grumbled among themselves, "This fellow moved into our city and now he acts like a judge. Let's treat him worse than his guests!"

The Sodomites pushed so hard against Lot that they almost broke down the door. But the two angels reached out, pulled Lot to safety, and bolted the door. Then they blinded the Sodomites so they grew tired trying to find the door.

"Find your relatives in the city and get them out of here," the angels warned, "for we will destroy the city completely. Get your daughters, sons-in-law, sons, or other relatives away, for the cry of evil has grown loud to the Lord and He has sent us to destroy the city completely."

Shaped like a woman wrapped in her cloak, this salt pinnacle on the slope of a mountain near Sodom is sometimes identified as "Lot's wife."

Lot first went to the young men who were about to marry his daughters. "Get out of the city, for the Lord is about to destroy it," he warned. But the young men looked at him as though he were joking.

By dawn the angels began to insist that Lot get out of Sodom. "Take your wife and two daughters and get out of here!" the angels urged. "Otherwise you will be destroyed when the city is punished."

But Lot still lingered; so the angels seized his hand and the hands of his wife and daughters, for the Lord had compassion on them. The angels led Lot and his family outside the city.

"Now run for your lives!" one of the angels said. "Do not look behind you and do not stop in the valley. Escape to the mountains or you will be carried away with the destruction."

"Oh, please, no," Lot pleaded. "You have been gracious and kind to me, but if I escape to the mountains I am sure some harm will come to me there. Look, there is a small village over there. Please let me go there, for it is nearby. It is a small village, and my life will be spared there."

"Hurry then, escape to that village, for I cannot do anything until you are safe there," the angel said. The name of that village was Zoar, which meant "Little Village."

The sun was rising by the time Lot reached Zoar. When he had almost reached the village, the Lord began His destruction of Sodom and Gomorrah, raining fire and brimstone upon them. The Lord destroyed those cities, the valley, and the other cities and villages of the surrounding plain. Everything was destroyed, including people and plants.

Lot's wife was lingering behind him. Longingly she looked back at Sodom, and she became a pillar of salt.

Early that morning Abraham arose and hurried to the place where he had talked with the Lord. As he looked toward Sodom and Gomorrah and the land of the valley, he saw the smoke from the destruction rising like the smoke of a great furnace. But God had remembered Abraham's request and had rescued Lot from the cities He destroyed.

Later Lot left Zoar and went to the mountains with his two daughters. One day the older daughter spoke with the younger. "There is not a man in this part of the country that our father would permit us to marry," she said. "If we are to have children we must have them through our father and he will soon be too old. Let's get him drunk with wine and have children by him so that our family may continue."

Frozen into a pillar of salt, Lot's wife is left behind while her husband and daughters flee the destruction of Sodom.

The Dead Sea contains a thirty-percent concentration of mineral salts, six times the amount found in the world's oceans. No life can survive in its bitter, salty waters.

The water of the Dead Sea evaporates under the hot desert sun, leaving behind large stretches of salt flats.

Salt mountains range along the southwestern shore of the Dead Sea. Water running down the slopes of the mountains add to the salt content of the water.

So they gave their father wine that night until he was drunk. And the older daughter went and lay with her father. But Lot did not know when his older daughter came to him or when she left.

The next day the older daughter said to the younger, "Last night I lay with my father. Tonight we will give him wine again and you can lie with him so that our family will continue through him."

That night they made Lot drunk again so that he did not know when his younger daughter lay down or when she arose. Both daughters conceived this way. The older daughter had a son and called his name Moab. He became the ancestor of the Moabites. The younger daughter also had a son and called his name Ben-ammi. He became the ancestor of the people known as the Ammonites.

The land surrounding ancient Sodom is barren, reminding one of the lifeless landscape of the moon. In Abraham's time, it was "well-watered land" so the passing of time has treated it harshly.

BIBLE FOR DAILY LIVING

People Profiles
Look up "Lot" in a Bible dictionary. On a piece of paper, list the qualities of character that made up his personality. How would you describe Lot to someone who did not know about him? How would you compare Lot and his qualities of character to Abraham and his qualities of character? Compare Lot and Abraham as far as: (1) godliness; (2) generosity; (3) family guidance as seen through the character of wife and children; (4) choice of friends and neighbors.

Personal Checkup
Using the same list of qualities of character, check up on yourself to see how you compare to Abraham. How do you compare yourself to Abraham as far as: (1) godliness; (2) generosity; (3) family guidance as seen through the character of family members; (4) choice of friends and neighbors? How do you compare yourself on each of these as far as the standard you feel should be set for Christian conduct?

Something to Think About
It is always helpful to compare or contrast ourselves with others to see how we measure up on certain matters. But it is more helpful to compare or contrast ourselves to the standards which we find in the Bible. It is worthwhile to list some of those standards and use them as a time of checking up.

Prayer Pointers
Help me find the right yardstick, Lord, when I would measure how I should live. May I follow no footsteps which would lead me away from You or the path where You want me to walk. And may the footsteps I leave behind me be pleasing in Your sight as others follow in them.

The Land of Palestine

The land known as "the Holy Land" has changed names and borders many times since the days of Abraham. Israel, the Promised Land, Canaan, and Palestine are all familiar terms, describing generally the land shown on the map at the right.

From west to east, this land has a fascinating pattern, moving upward in steps until it drops abruptly into the Jordan River Valley on the eastern side, far below sea level.

The names for these various steps appear on the map at the right. Photos surrounding the map identify them today.

Starting at the west, the land begins at the shore of the Great Sea, now known as the Mediterranean Sea (two center photos, near right). Moving eastward, the next step upward is the broad, level Plain of Sharon (top photo, near right). Next comes the Shephelah, the lower foothills (lower photo, near right). After that, the hill country, a mountainous region stretching from north to south (second photo from bottom, far right).

From these mountains, the land drops to the Jordan River Valley, with the Dead Sea at the southern end (bottom picture, far right) and the Sea of Galilee (second from top, far right) and Galilee (top, far right) at the northern end.

These steps are interrupted in the north by a great valley (right center photo, far right), known as the Jezreel Valley, Plain of Megiddo, or the Plain of Esdraelon. In the south they are interrupted by a great wilderness known as the Negeb, gentle in the west (below map, left) and rugged in the east (below map, right).

Human Failings

It is a mistake to think of Bible heroes as different from men and women today. Even those with towering faith still had human failings. Abraham's weakness was fear. Again we see Abraham lie about his relationship with Sarah. Why? "I thought these people did not fear God at all." The people of the land might not know God, but God was there. And His power was unlimited.

Abraham Deceives Abimelech
From Genesis 20

Later Abraham left Mamre and moved southward again to the Negeb, settling between Kadesh and Shur. On a visit to Gerar, Abraham said that Sarah was his sister so Abimelech the king of Gerar sent for her.

But God appeared to Abimelech in a dream that night. "You are marked for death because you have taken that man's wife," God told him.

At this time Abimelech had not even come near Sarah. "Lord, will You destroy innocent people?" he asked. "Didn't Abraham tell me that she was his sister? And didn't she say that he was her brother? My heart and hands are clean in this matter."

"I know that you are innocent," God continued in the dream. "But it is I Who restrained you from touching her. Now give her back to her husband, for he is a prophet. He will pray for you and you will live. If you do not return her, you and your household are marked for death."

When Abimelech arose in the morning, he told his servants about the dream and they were very frightened. Abimelech called for Abraham to talk with him.

"What have you done to us?" he demanded. "And what sin have I committed against you to cause you to bring this upon me and my kingdom? What you have done is very wrong! Why did you do it?"

"I thought that you people did not fear God and that you would kill me because of my wife," Abraham answered. "She is my sister, for she is my father's daughter, but not my mother's. But she is also my wife. When God caused me to travel far away from my father's land, I asked her to show kindness to me by saying that I am her brother."

Then Abimelech gave Abraham sheep, oxen, and male and female servants, and he returned Sarah his wife to him also.

"You may settle anywhere you wish in my land," said Abimelech.

To Sarah he said, "I have given your brother a thousand pieces of silver. It will compensate you for whatever trouble I have caused you and your family. You are clear now before all men."

Abimelech was frightened by the thought of the sin he might have committed and angry at Abraham for not telling him the whole truth.

Then Abraham prayed to God and He healed Abimelech and his wife and the other women around them, so they could have children again. For the Lord had caused all of these women to be barren as long as Sarah remained in Abimelech's household.

Tell Abu Hureirah has been identified as the ancient city of Gerar. During much of its history the city was occupied by the Philistines. The mound is located about fifteen miles northwest of Beer-sheba.

BIBLE FOR DAILY LIVING

Bible Quiz

The following facts help us remember important parts of the life of Abraham:

1. Abraham bargained with the Lord to spare Sodom. At last the Lord said He would spare Sodom if He could find how many righteous men in it?
   a. 10   b. 20   c. 30
2. When some angels visited Lot's house in Sodom, the people of the village
   a. received them as good hosts   b. received them with evil actions
3. When Lot escaped from Sodom, his wife was
   a. destroyed in the fire   b. turned to a pillar of salt   c. rescued
4. Lot and his daughters escaped to
   a. Mamre   b. Jerusalem   c. Zoar
5. Lot's older daughter had a son who became the ancestor of the
   a. Moabites   b. Ammonites   c. Israelites
6. Abraham lied to Abimelech, telling him that Sarah was his
   a. wife   b. daughter   c. sister
7. Abimelech was king of
   a. Hebron   b. Gerar   c. Mamre
8. Sarah was not only Abraham's wife but also his
   a. father's daughter   b. mother's daughter

Answers: 1a, 2b, 3b, 4c, 5a, 6c, 7b, 8a

Prayer Pointers

Guard my lips, O Lord, that I may tell the whole truth, even when I know it will hurt.

These Sumerian statuettes date back to the time of Abraham. They served as stand-ins for worshipers who could not be present in the temple.

This frieze, discovered at Ur, shows ancient Sumerians milking their herds.

Nippur (above) was one of the leading cities of Sumer, Abraham's homeland. The remains of this ancient city are surrounded by a sea of sand.

The Journeys of Abraham and Isaac

The journeys of Abraham and Isaac were not tourist trips for pleasure and sight-seeing, but migrations of a tribal leader with his people. Often these were ordered by God.

Abraham's journeys, as recorded in the Bible, began at his hometown of Ur, then part of Sumer. At God's command, he and his family went up through the Tigris and Euphrates River Valleys to Haran. After some time at Haran, Abraham left for Canaan, where he stayed first at Shechem, in the Plain of Moreh.

Bethel was Abraham's next stop, and then "the south," the Negeb. But a famine forced him to leave with Sarah and his family for Egypt. After a short stay in Egypt, they returned to Canaan, living first at Bethel, then at Mamre, then Gerar, and finally at Beer-sheba.

Abraham made one other journey, far to the north to Hobah, near Damascus. There he and a select band of armed men defeated a raiding party led by four kings from the north, rescuing Lot. He returned past Salem, which is

modern Jerusalem, and gave a tenth of the spoils to its king, who was also a priest.

The travels of Abraham's son Isaac were much more restrictive. As the solid line on the map shows, Isaac never left the general area of his birth. Gerar, Beer-sheba, and Beer-lahai-roi were the three principal places on his itinerary.

When one realizes that journeys such as these meant the movement of herds and flocks, tents and children, often on foot, it is not surprising that people went so seldom.

Dotted lines trace the course of Abraham's travels in the land of Canaan. Isaac's route is marked in solid lines.

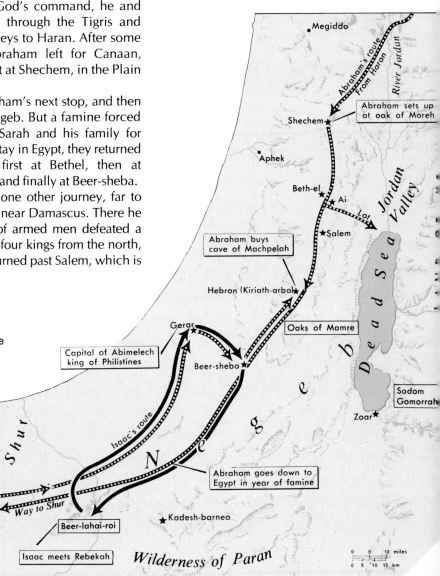

Scenes from the days of the patriarchs continue to live in the Bedouin marketplace. Left: a young man tends his camel.

Below: a camel in full harness waits for its rider. The covered saddle is used by Bedouin women to shade them from the heat of the desert sun. A man's saddle lacks this protective canopy.

Everyone takes part in the job of setting up camp. The men supervise while the women and children pitch the tent. The cloth stretched on the ground (right) will be hung between the men's and women's sections of the tent.

Family Friction

Years before the birth of Sarah's miracle child, Isaac, she had given a young Egyptian servant woman to Abraham as a second wife. When a boy, Ishmael, was born, Sarah claimed him as her own. There was always jealousy between the two women. But after Isaac's birth, the friction grew. "Throw out the slave woman and her child," Sarah demanded. Abraham refused. But God directed Abraham to do as Sarah asked. "I will make a great nation from Ishmael as well as from Isaac," God promised. So with only a pot of water, Ishmael and his mother went into the wilderness. Today the Arab peoples trace their line back to this outcast boy.

Abraham Sends Hagar into the Wilderness
From Genesis 21

The Lord remembered His promise to Sarah and gave her and Abraham a son, even though they were both too old to have a child naturally. It happened at the time God had said it would.

Abraham named his new son Isaac, which meant "Laughter." When Isaac was eight days old, Abraham circumcised him as God had commanded. At this time, Abraham was a hundred years old.

"God has brought laughter to me," said Sarah, "for whoever hears of this will laugh with me. Who would have thought that Abraham and I would have a child at this age? Yet here I am, nursing a child when I am old!"

As time passed the child Isaac grew and was weaned. On the day he was weaned, Abraham gave a great feast. But Sarah noticed that Ishmael, son of Abraham and Hagar the Egyptian, was mocking Isaac.

"Drive Hagar and her son away from us!" Sarah demanded. "I will not have that woman's child become an heir with my son Isaac."

This disturbed Abraham greatly, for Ishmael was his son. But the Lord said to Abraham, "Don't be disturbed because of Hagar and Ishmael. Do what Sarah tells you, for My covenant is through Isaac, and through him your name will remain throughout history. But I will make a great nation through Ishmael also, for he is your descendant."

Early the next morning Abraham prepared some food and a skin filled with water for Hagar, put them on her shoulder and sent her away with Ishmael. But she had nowhere to go, and she wandered in the Wilderness of Beer-sheba.

When the water was gone, Hagar placed Ishmael under a bush and sat down about a hundred yards away. "I do not want to watch him die," Hagar cried out. Then she began to cry, wailing loudly.

God heard Ishmael's cries and the Angel of God called out to Hagar from heaven. "What is the trouble, Hagar," the Angel said. "You must not be afraid, for God has heard Ishmael's cries as he lies there. Now go and pick up the boy and hold his hand, for I will make a great nation from him."

Then God opened Hagar's eyes so that she noticed a well of water. She filled the animal skin with water and gave Ishmael some to drink.

In early times Beer-sheba was only a watering stop in the open desert. Later it grew into a city, for people settled wherever they could find a source of water. The scenes above show the wilderness area surrounding Beer-sheba today.

God was with Ishmael as he grew up in the wilderness of Paran with his mother. When the time came for Ishmael to marry, Hagar arranged for him to take a wife from Egypt.

About that same time King Abimelech and his army commander, Phicol, visited Abraham. "God is with you in everything you do," he said. "Swear to me by God that you will never deal falsely with me or my son or grandson, and that you will remain friendly to me and my country where you have come to live as a stranger, as I have been friendly to you."

"I swear it," Abraham replied.

But Abraham complained to Abimelech about a well of water which Abimelech's servants had taken by force. "I

While she sat in the wilderness near Beer-sheba, watching her son die of thirst, Hagar heard the voice of the Lord call to her, promising her that this son would not die but become the father of a great nation.

never knew this happened," said Abimelech. "I don't know who did it, and you did not tell me about it. Today is the first time I heard about it."

Then Abraham gave some sheep and oxen to Abimelech, and the two of them made a covenant. But when he set aside seven ewe lambs by themselves, Abimelech asked, "What do these seven ewe lambs mean, which you set aside from the others?"

"These lambs are my gift to you, to witness to all here that I dug this well," Abraham answered.

Tradition claims this well in modern Beer-sheba as the well of Abraham. It may have been one of his wells, but ancient Beer-sheba, where Abraham lived, was several miles to the northeast.

Thus Abraham named the place Beer-sheba, which meant "Well of the Covenant" for that was the place where he and Abimelech made their covenant. Then Abimelech and Phicol arose and returned home to the land of the Philistines.

Abraham planted a tamarisk tree at Beer-sheba and called upon the name of the Lord, the Everlasting God. For a long time Abraham remained there in the land of the Philistines.

BIBLE FOR DAILY LIVING

Bible Truth in Action

The origin of Beer-sheba's name is in this reading. It came from the uneasy truce which Abraham and Abimelech made. Abimelech recognized that Abraham had become quite wealthy, and therefore powerful. Concerned that Abraham might some day turn this power against him or his descendants, Abimelech asked Abraham for a treaty. Abraham agreed, but took this occasion to complain about the theft of a well. Not content with complaining about it, Abraham made his complaint dramatic by setting aside seven ewe lambs. The account never tells whether Abraham got his well back or not, but years later, Isaac had trouble with these same people concerning some of the same wells. The covenant was that Abraham and Abimelech would be friendly, not necessarily friends. They would not go to war, but that did not force them to be generous or kind to one another. This uneasy truce exists between many individuals today—friendly, but not truly friends.

Words and Meanings

Isaac was born among troubled circumstances. Rushing ahead of God's promises, Sarah had given her servant girl Hagar to Abraham as a second wife so that she would produce the promised heir. As might be expected, this also produced jealousy and hatred between Sarah and Hagar. Then at last Sarah's son was born and things came to a head between the two women. Isaac, whose name meant "Laughter" was clearly in competition with Ishmael, whose name meant "God Heard." For Sarah, the name of Isaac meant that others would laugh for joy with Sarah because the long-promised son had arrived. For Hagar, the name of her son Ishmael meant that God had heard her in her time of affliction. What would Hagar and Sarah have thought if they could have looked across the years and seen Ishmael's descendants carrying Sarah's great-grandson Joseph to Egypt as a slave? Sarah may have stopped her laughter for a moment to shed some tears while Hagar may have stopped her tears for a moment of laughter.

Today Beer-sheba is a modern city with a large population. Nearby, tamarisk trees, like the one Abraham planted, still grow.

The Desert

Sand and sea continually wrestle for control of Palestine. Cool winds blowing from the west bring life-giving rain from the Mediterranean Sea. From mid-October through the first half of May these moisture-laden breezes water the earth. But as the month of May gives way to June the winds shift and the temperature rises sharply. Dry hot winds begin to blow from the desert, sometimes bringing clouds of dust.

The people of Bible lands have given a name to the scorching wind. They call it the "Sirocco," which means "the easterner." But despite its name, this dreaded wind does not always come from across the Jordan. Palestine is bordered on two sides by the vast Arabian desert, and the desert winds blow their hot breath from the south as well as the east.

Like a grasping hand, the Sirocco reaches over the borders of Palestine, drawing the margins of the land into the desert's domain. In some portions of Palestine the desert has made serious inroads into the land. In the southern region of Israel, called the Negeb, the dry touch of the desert reaches into the territory of Judah. The Rift Valley and the

11

The austere landscape of the desert dominates the Sinai Peninsula. Although daytime temperatures during the summer months regularly climb over the one-hundred-degree mark, nighttime temperatures may be as much as thirty degrees cooler. Annual rainfall in this parched wilderness amounts to less than one inch.

Dead Sea basin are also dominated by the harsh desert climate.

Although the desert winds would bring death to a farmer's fields, the arid climate means home to the nomad. His herds feed on the tough vegetation that clings stubbornly to the low, rolling hills. Pitching his tent wherever he can find water, he follows his herds from place to place.

The nomad's existence is a constant battle against the harsh desert climate. In years of drought he is the first to suffer from the lack of rain. During Bible times hungry nomadic desert tribes often raided Israel's borders for food and water.

With its vast stretches of uninhabited land, the desert was also a refuge for criminals. Bands of roving thieves attacked caravans traveling the ancient trade routes. The rocky region east of the Jordan was filled with caves that offered sheltered hiding places to the desert outlaws.

The parched landscape of the desert was broken only by an occasional oasis. In a few areas underground springs supplied enough water to support tropical plant life. These green islands in a sea of sand made welcome rest stops for weary travelers.

Although modern methods of irrigation have reclaimed portions of the desert, most of it has remained unchanged since Bible times. Just as in Abraham's day, empty stretches of barren land reach as far as the eye can see.

Although the desert may appear to be a barren wasteland, untapped treasures of mineral wealth are contained in its hills. Geologists report significant deposits of copper, iron, and manganese. Quantities of salt, gypsum, and natural gas have been discovered as well. Modern technology is constantly searching for more efficient methods of mining these minerals. Desert regions shown at the top, left to right: Judean Desert, Judean Desert near Jericho, a desert patrol in Jordan. At the bottom, left to right: Sinai Desert, wilderness near Jericho, and the Wadi Arabah.

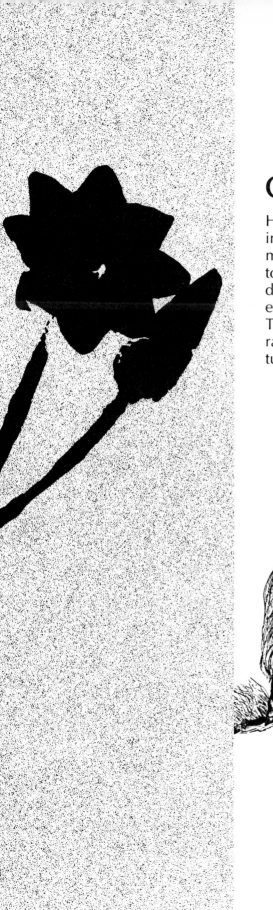

God Will Provide

Human sacrifice, although sometimes practiced in Abraham's day, was forbidden by God. What must Abraham have thought when God told him to sacrifice Isaac, the child through whom his descendants were to come? Abraham obeyed . . . expecting God to somehow keep His promise. Then, at the place of sacrifice, God did provide. A ram, caught by its horns in a thicket, was substituted on the altar for Isaac.

This five-thousand-year-old sculpture of a ram in a thicket was discovered in the royal tombs of Ur. It is made of wood overlaid with gold and adorned with lapis lazuli.

Abraham met God's test with perfect faith. When the Lord commanded him to offer his only son, the child of his old age, Abraham did not hesitate to obey.

Abraham Offers Isaac
From Genesis 22

One day God arranged a test for Abraham, to see if he would trust and obey God no matter what He asked him to do.

"Abraham!" God called.

"I am here," Abraham answered.

"Take your only son Isaac, whom you love dearly, to the land of Moriah and offer him there as a burnt offering on the mountain I will show you," the Lord said.

Early the next morning Abraham saddled his donkey, split the wood for the burnt offering, and left for Moriah with Isaac and two servants. On the third day, Abraham saw Moriah from a distance.

"Stay here with the donkey," Abraham told the two young servants. "Isaac and I will go over there to worship, and we will return."

Abraham put the wood for the fire on Isaac's shoulders while he carried the torch and knife. Then the two of them set out together for Moriah.

"My father," said Isaac.

"Yes, I am here," Abraham answered.

"I see the torch and the wood, but where is the lamb for the burnt offering?" Isaac inquired.

"God Himself will provide the lamb for the burnt offering, my son," Abraham said.

The two walked on together until they came to the place which God had told him about. Abraham built an altar there and arranged the wood on it. He bound his son Isaac and laid him on top of the wood. Then he took the knife and prepared to kill Isaac with it.

But as Abraham was ready to plunge the knife into Isaac, the Angel of the Lord called to him from heaven. "Abraham! Abraham!" the Angel called.

"Here I am," said Abraham.

"Do not harm the lad," the Angel said. "Now I know for sure that you trust God completely, for you have not held back one thing in your life, not even your only son whom you love so much."

When Abraham looked up, he saw a ram caught in the thicket by its horns. He took the ram and offered it for a burnt offering instead of his son.

Abraham called that place Jehovah-jireh, which meant "The Lord Will Provide." It was still called that at the time this was written.

Tradition has identified the temple mount in Jerusalem as Mount Moriah, the scene of Abraham's sacrifice.

Inside the Dome of the Rock the stony peak of the mountain juts through the floor of the shrine. According to tradition, this was the place where Abraham prepared to sacrifice his son Isaac.

154

Once again the Angel of the Lord called from heaven. "I have sworn by Myself that because you have followed My command exactly and did not withhold even your only son, I will bless you greatly and will multiply your descendants as the stars of the heavens and the sand of the seashore; and your descendants will conquer their enemies and will bless all the nations of the earth, for you have obeyed Me."

Then Abraham and Isaac returned to the two servants, and they traveled back to Beer-sheba. Abraham made his home there at Beer-sheba for a while.

About that same time Abraham heard that his brother Nahor and his wife Milcah had eight sons. Their names were Uz, Buz, Kemuel the father of Aram, Chesed, Hazo, Pildash, Jidlaph, and Bethuel, who became the father of Rebekah.

Nahor had other children by his concubine Reumah. They were Tebah, Gaham, Tahash, and Maacah.

Jewish legend claims that Solomon built the Holy of Holies over the exact rock where Abraham built his altar on Mount Moriah.

BIBLE FOR DAILY LIVING

Bible Truth in Action

Abraham is known for his deep and unfailing trust, or faith, in God. Never was this more severely tested than in the event described in this reading. Until the time when he was one hundred years old, Abraham had waited for the birth of his promised son Isaac. Thus Isaac became a very special person to Abraham and his wife Sarah. Abraham would have let nothing take Isaac from him—no enemy could have fought for him, no price could have purchased him, no force could have been powerful enough to have torn Isaac from him. But when God told Abraham to sacrifice his son, Abraham proceeded to do it without question. That is total obedience. It should be noted also that Isaac did not resist his father, for he also trusted God completely, even at this early age. True faith knows no limits.

Personal Enrichment

The place where Abraham prepared to sacrifice Isaac was Mount Moriah. Look up "Moriah" in a Bible dictionary to learn more about the mountain. Later, Solomon built his temple here. In the time of Jesus, Herod's temple stood at the same place. Look up "temple" also in a Bible dictionary to see the history of the temple built on this mountain. Today the "Dome of the Rock" stands on this same mountain. Moriah is one peak in the same mountain range in which Calvary was located. Thus Abraham prepared to sacrifice his beloved son in the same mountain range as God sacrificed His beloved Son. Abraham was the central figure in the old covenant; Jesus was the central figure in the new covenant.

The Mountains of the Land

From north to south, a range of mountains formed a backbone through the central part of Palestine. These mountains played an important part in the history of Israel.

In time of war, the mountains became a natural defense. It was almost impossible, and certainly not effective, for chariots to be used in these mountains. Chariots were made for battle in the broad plains.

The mountains mentioned in the Bible remain today as continuing landmarks, outliving man-made cities, towns and buildings. Names of mountains remain much the same throughout Bible history, and even until modern times.

Foreign religions often crowned a mountain or hill with a pagan temple or shrine, dedicated to a heathen god. At low points in their history, Israelites joined their neighbors to worship these pagan gods in the mountains.

In the days of the Hebrew kings, high places were erected where the Israelites went to sacrifice or worship God. Perhaps Israelites and Canaanites wanted to take their worship as close to heaven as possible.

God often revealed Himself upon a mountain. He made His promise to Noah on Mount Ararat and confirmed Abraham's faith in Him on Mount Moriah. Moses received the law on Mount Sinai and Jesus was transfigured on Mount Hermon or Mount Tabor.

Thus the mountains were vital to the people, in war, in worship, and in daily living.

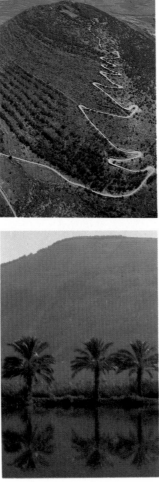

In the top row of pictures, from left to right: Lebanon Mountains, a winding road up Mount Tabor, Mount Carmel, mountains of Edom. In the bottom row from left to right: Mount Hermon, Mount Gilboa, eastern Mount Carmel, mountains of Judah and the mountains of Ephraim. Above: mountains of Judah.

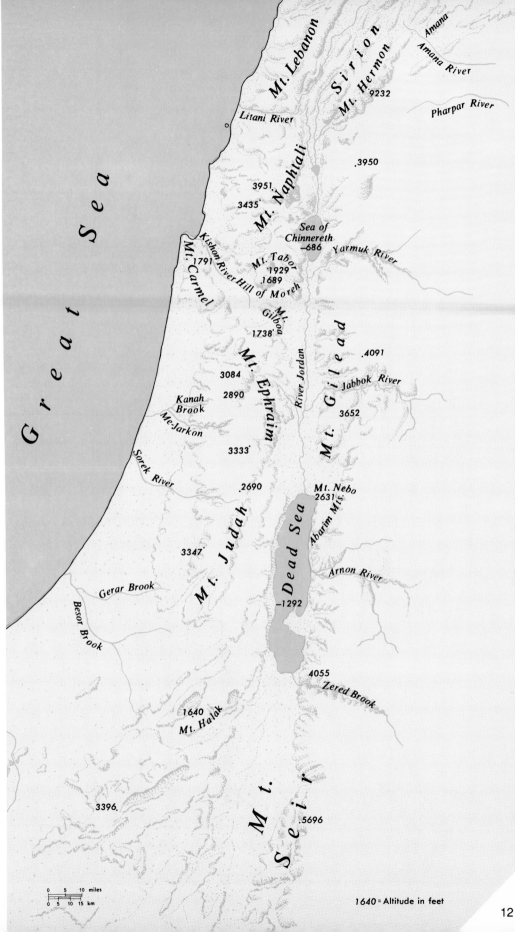

Mt. Lebanon

Sirion

Amana

Mt. Hermon
.9232

Amana River

Litani River

Pharpar River

Great Sea

.3950

Mt. Naphtali

3951.

3435.

Sea of Chinnereth
−686

Yarmuk River

Kishon River

Mt. Carmel

.1791

Mt. Tabor
.1929
.1689
Hill of Moreh

Mt. Gilboa

1738.

.4091

Mt. Gilead

River Jordan

Jabbok River

3084.

2890.

Mt. Ephraim

3652.

Kanah Brook

Me-Jarkon

3333.

Sorek River

.2690

Mt. Nebo
2631.

Abarim Mts.

Mt. Judah

Dead Sea
−1292

Arnon River

3347.

Gerar Brook

Besor Brook

4055.

Zered Brook

1640
Mt. Halak

3396.

Mt. Seir

.5696

0   5   10 miles
0 5 10 15 km

1640 = Altitude in feet

12

Sarah's Death

Sarah lived to see her son Isaac become a man. When she died, Abraham bargained for a choice burial place. The people with whom he bargained, the Hittites, and the very location, the cave at Machpelah, are both well known today. Abraham weighed out the purchase price on scales something like those shown here. Sorrowing, he laid his wife to rest. One generation had passed. The story of God's people would now continue in Abraham and Sarah's son.

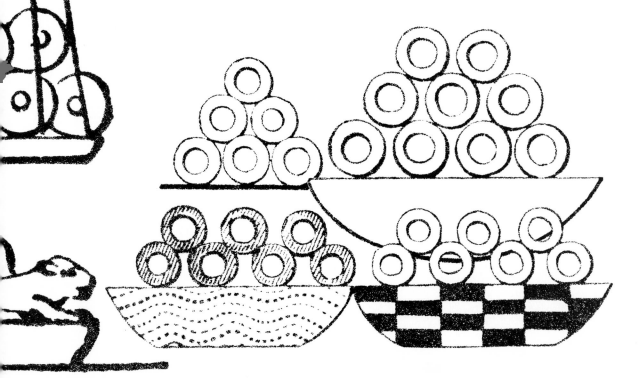

A large Moslem mosque stands over the cave of Machpelah. Abraham bought the tomb for his wife and was later buried here himself. The mouth of the cave is at the far right, but no one is permitted to enter it.

Sarah Dies and Is Buried
From Genesis 23

Sarah died at the age of a hundred and twenty-seven at Kiriath-arba, known also as Hebron; and Abraham mourned and wept for her there. Then he stood up from his mourning to speak with the sons of Heth.

"I am a stranger here, but I would like to bury my dead in this place," he told them. "I would like to buy a burial place from you."

"You are one of God's princes, living here among us," they answered. "Choose the best of our sepulchers and not one of us will refuse to let you have it."

Abraham bowed low before the Hittites, the people of that land, and said to them, "If you will let me bury my dead among you, ask Ephron, Zohar's son, to sell me the cave of Machpelah at the end of his field. I will pay the full price for it so that I may have it for my family cemetery."

Ephron was sitting there with his neighbors so he answered Abraham in the presence of the other Hittites gathered at the city gate. "Let me give you the field, my lord, and the cave that is in it," he said. "In the presence of all my people, I give it to you. Go and bury your dead."

Abraham bowed before the people of the land. "Listen to me," he said. "I will give you the full price for the field. Accept it so that I may bury my dead."

"My lord," Ephron replied. "The land is worth four hundred pieces of silver. But what is that between me and you?"

In the presence of the other Hittites, Abraham weighed out the amount Ephron had stated in the money used by the merchants. So Abraham legally bought the field with the cave, and all the trees in the field to its boundaries. The sale was witnessed by the Hittites who gathered at the city gate, and the land became Abraham's.

Then Abraham buried Sarah his wife in the cave of the field at Machpelah, near Mamre at Hebron, in the land of Canaan. The field and the cave in it were deeded by the sons of Heth to Abraham for a burial site, a permanent family cemetery.

Abraham and Ephron the Hittite bargained according to the custom of the ancient Near East. When the sale was agreed upon, Abraham weighed out four hundred shekels of silver.

Together Sarah and Abraham had left their home in Ur to follow God's direction.
Now Abraham is alone. He turns back for one last look before Sarah's tomb is sealed.
Below right: Hebron, with the mosque over the cave at Machpelah in the center.

An unbroken seal on the entrance of a tomb was evidence that the grave had not been disturbed by robbers.
These seals are Akkadian and are of the cylinder-seal variety.

BIBLE FOR DAILY LIVING

Bible Quiz
Review what you have learned during the last three readings. This quiz is concerned with some of the major events in the life of Abraham:
1. When Isaac was born, Abraham was how old?
   a. 80   b. 90   c. 100
2. Ishmael's mother was
   a. Hagar   b. Sarah   c. Keturah
3. Abimelech was a
   a. Hittite   b. Philistine   c. Israelite
4. When Sarah died, Abraham bought a cave named
   a. Hebron   b. Kiriath-arba   c. Machpelah
5. For this cave, Abraham paid how many pieces of silver?
   a. 100   b. 400   c. 1000
6. Abraham prepared to sacrifice Isaac on Mount
   a. Moriah   b. Sinai   c. Tabor
7. When Hagar and Ishmael were sent away into the wilderness, Ishmael
   a. died   b. almost died, but was spared by God

Answers: 1c, 2a, 3b, 4c, 5b, 6a, 7b

Something to Think About
Imagine what must have gone through Abraham's mind as he buried Sarah in the cave at Machpelah. He surely must have reflected back over all the events that they had shared together. Can you name several of them? And he must have thought also of all the qualities that made Sarah precious to him. Can you name some of Sarah's qualities of character, as shown in her various activities? You may also discover a few qualities that were not so endearing. As in most Bible-time people, these showed the human side of that person's life.

Prayer Pointers
Lord, help me evaluate the past as I search for guidelines to the future. May I discover in the failures of others my own tendency to fail and in their successes, how I may overcome.

Old Age

Commercials and advertisements everywhere in today's civilized world loudly proclaim their products' ability to turn back the hands of time. They promise the buyer a new and years-younger appearance with powders, creams, dyes, clothes, makeup and even perfume.

The ancient Israelites would have been amused at this modern quest for eternal youth. In Bible times old age was considered a blessing from God and gray hair was a badge of honor. Every man desired a long life and the respect from others that came with it. Young people looked to the old for wisdom and guidance. Positions of leadership were entrusted to the aged.

In the early chapters of Genesis the people of ancient times lived to a great old age. A single lifetime might span almost a thousand years in the days before the Great Flood. Methuselah, the oldest man in the Bible, is described as having lived to be nine hundred and sixty-nine years old.

After Noah, the human life span gradually declined. By the time of Abraham, two hundred years had become the limit of a long life. Isaac, the oldest of the patriarchs, lived to be one hundred and eighty years old, but his grandson, Joseph, died at the age of one hundred and ten.

Because they lived longer, Bible-time men and women married late in life. Many people today marry in their late teens or early twenties, but some of these men married anywhere from forty to ninety. Esau took his Hittite wives at the age of forty, and his twin brother Jacob was over eighty before he married Rachel and Leah.

In ancient times the wife was often much younger than her husband. A man wanted to marry a young woman so that she could bear him many sons. But the strain and dangers of childbirth cut short the life span of many Old Testament women. Rachel, Jacob's favorite wife, died after the birth of Benjamin.

For the man or woman who survived the years, old age brought the respect of their juniors. But the passing of time then, as now, also meant the decline of physical strength. The writer of Ecclesiastes mourned the weakening eyesight and the loss of vigor that accompany old age. Human disabilities like these plagued even the great personalities of the Old Testament. Isaac and Jacob were hindered by blindness and King David suffered from poor circulation in his last years.

With the lack of proper medicine and health care, it is somewhat amazing that anyone lived to old age. No wonder they were honored so much by the young!

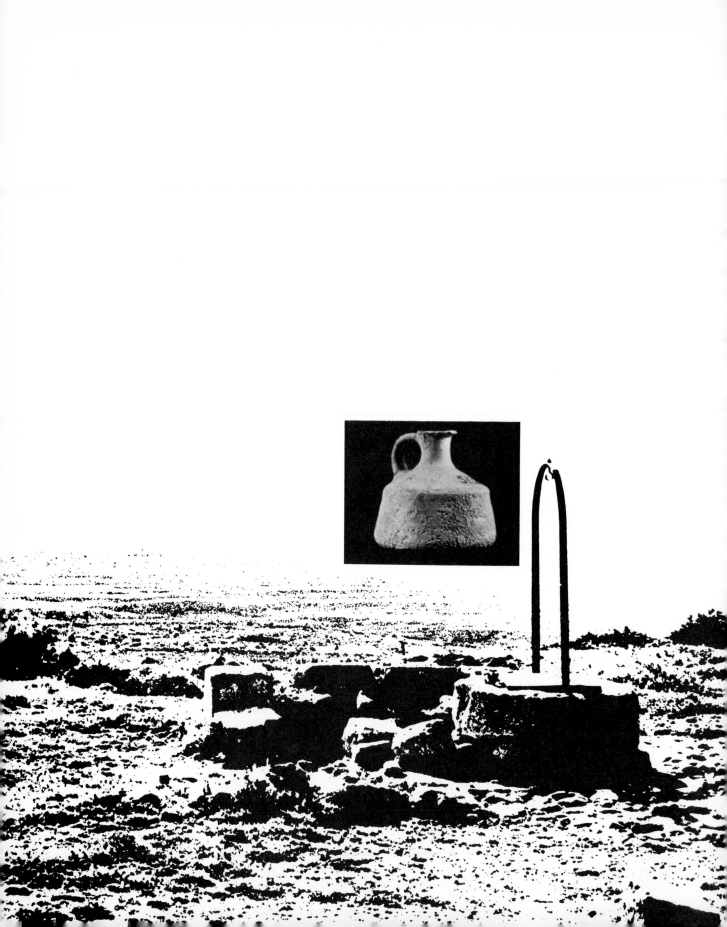

Choice of a Wife

God had chosen Isaac to inherit His promises to Abraham. Could the choice of Isaac's wife be unimportant? The Bible tells the story of the search for Isaac's wife. It is a story of answered prayer beside a well, and of God's arrangement of every detail.

A Bride for Isaac
From Genesis 24:1-33

Abraham had grown very old, and God continued to bless him in every way. But Abraham became concerned about Isaac and called his oldest servant who was in charge of his household.

"Place your hand under my thigh and swear by the Lord, the God of heaven and earth, that you will not permit my son to marry one of the Canaanite neighbor girls," Abraham commanded. "You must return to my country and to my family and find a wife for Isaac among them."

"But what if she will not come back here with me?" the servant asked. "Shall I take Isaac there?"

"Beware of taking Isaac there," Abraham warned. "The Lord, the God of heaven, Who took me from my father's household and the land of my birth and made a covenant with me said He would give this land to my descendants. He will send His angel before you so that you may find a wife for Isaac. But if the woman is not willing to come back here, you are free from your oath to me. Even then, you must not take Isaac to that land."

When Rebekah willingly offered to draw water for Eliezer and his ten thirsty camels, the old servant knew that he had found the girl chosen by God to be Isaac's bride.

The servant placed his hand under Abraham's thigh and swore that he would do as Abraham had told him. Then he took ten of Abraham's camels and set out for the city of Nahor in Mesopotamia with many valuable gifts from Abraham.

The servant arrived at Nahor one evening, at the time when the young women of the city came out to draw water. He had his camels kneel by the well and there he prayed.

"O Lord, God of my master Abraham, help my journey to be successful today and thus show kindness to my master Abraham," he prayed. "I stand here by this well of water as the young women of the city come out to draw water. When I ask for a drink, may Isaac's wife be the one who offers to draw water for my camels also. By this I will know that You have shown favor to my master."

Before the servant had finished praying, a young woman came out to the well with a water jar on her shoulder. She was Rebekah, the daughter of Bethuel and granddaughter of Abraham's brother Nahor and his wife Milcah.

Rebekah, a very beautiful virgin girl, went to the well to fill her jar with water. When she left the well, the servant ran to meet her.

Camels are often called the "ships of the desert." They can store enough water in their humps to supply their bodies' needs for three or four days of desert travel. Eliezer needed such animals for his long journey.

The average camel can carry a load of four hundred pounds and cover a distance of twenty-eight miles in a day.

Today the sun sets over a silent landscape, but in Abraham's lifetime Haran was an important center of trade.

"Please may I have a drink from your jar?" he asked.

"Drink, my lord," Rebekah replied. She lowered her jar of water to her hand for him to drink.

"I'll draw enough water for your camels, too," she offered.

Rebekah emptied her jar of water into the trough and ran back to the well to draw more water for the camels. The servant watched her until she was finished, for he was anxious to know if this was the young woman the Lord had in mind for Isaac.

When the camels had had enough to drink the servant brought out a golden nose ring weighing a half-shekel (about a quarter of an ounce) and two golden bracelets weighing ten shekels (about five ounces).

Sheltered from the desert sun, Bedouin men relax inside their tent, much like the men of Jacob's time would have done.

"Whose daughter are you?" he asked. "Is there room in your father's house for us to stay tonight?"

"I am the daughter of Bethuel, the son of Nahor and Milcah," she answered. "We have plenty of straw and feed and room where you can stay."

The servant bowed low and worshiped the Lord. "Blessed be the Lord, the God of my master Abraham," he prayed. "You have remembered him with lovingkindness and truth, for You have guided me to the house of my master's family."

Rebekah ran home to tell her mother's household what had happened. When her brother Laban heard what Rebekah said and saw the golden ring and bracelets, he ran out to find the man, who was standing by his camels at the well.

"Come home with me!" Laban invited. "Don't stand here by the well. We have a room for you and a place for the camels."

Abraham's servant went home with Laban, who unloaded the camels and gave them straw and feed. Laban also gave the man water to wash his feet and the feet of the men with him.

But when food was brought before him, the man refused to eat. "I must first tell you why I have come," he said.

"Speak," said Laban. "Tell us what you wish."

BIBLE FOR DAILY LIVING

Bible Truth in Action

The Lord guides in ways beyond human understanding. The incident of Eliezer searching for a bride for Isaac is one example. Note: (1) Eliezer prayed that the Lord would make his journey successful; (2) he prayed specifically that the girl of the Lord's choosing would give his camels water; and (3) he recognized the Lord's answer to his prayers. Remember that Eliezer was on a mission for Abraham and Isaac, not for himself. Remember also that he knew that the God of Abraham would lead him to the right person, His choice for Isaac's bride. With that unswerving faith, Eliezer dared to pray for a miracle, and also dared to accept it when the Lord sent it. Is it possible that we miss many miracles the Lord would send because we fail to pray for them, fail to believe that the Lord will send them, fail to recognize them when they come, and even fail to accept what He sends?

Personal Checkup

Think about the two greatest needs in your life today. Does it seem that only a miracle will supply them? What have you learned from the above to guide you in seeking God's answer to your needs? How might you approach your greatest needs now? Be sure to ask: (1) Would supplying these needs be pleasing to the Lord, in harmony with His will? (2) Are these truly needs and not merely wants? (3) Would having these needs supplied bring you nearer to the Lord, or take you farther from Him? Unanswered prayer may be God's answer, "This is not good for you." If answered prayer is in His will, it may come as a miracle.

Prayer Pointers

Lord, I pray for Your will to be done in my life, not that my wants shall be supplied. I ask for You to supply every need, according to Your riches, but to deny those things which will divert my affection from You. When I pray for something that is not pleasing to You, answer "no." But when I seek what You know I should have, work wonders to perform it in my life.

These stones mark the site of an ancient well outside the village of Haran. In Bible times the town well was a popular meeting place for women who came daily to draw water.

A Bedouin woman in the marketplace wears heavy ornaments of silver and gold.

Jewelry

The love of jewelry is as old as mankind itself. Even before the discovery of precious metals, people made ornaments from objects found in nature. Early men wore necklaces of rocks, shells, animal bones and teeth. But as ancient craftsmen developed skill in metalworking, they learned to fashion ornaments of gold. Soft and flexible, it was easily hammered into a variety of shapes, and its rich shining luster appealed to a love of color.

Jewelry was valued for more than its beauty as an ornament. It was also used as a form of money in the ancient world. Before the invention of coins, gold and silver were weighed and their value exactly measured; an object could be literally "worth its weight in gold" on a merchant's scale. Precious metals could be used to purchase a plot of land, buy a slave or pay taxes to the king.

Precious stones were also used in trade. Not only were they admired for their brilliance and color, but they were also valued for their supposed magic powers. People in ancient times were convinced that certain stones could ward off disease or drive away evil spirits. They believed that a diamond guaranteed victory for a soldier, while an emerald protected its owner from the magician's evil spell. Amethysts were valued as a cure for drunkenness, and the effects of poisons were thought to be counteracted by sapphires.

The people of ancient times believed that the magic powers of these gems were so strong that they could affect life beyond the grave, and the dead were buried with their jewels as protection against dangers in the afterlife. Many beautifully crafted pieces of jewelry have been discovered in the pyramids of the Egyptian pharaohs and in the royal tombs at Ur.

Aristocratic ladies in ancient Ur wore hairnets of woven ribbon wreathed with circlets of golden leaves.

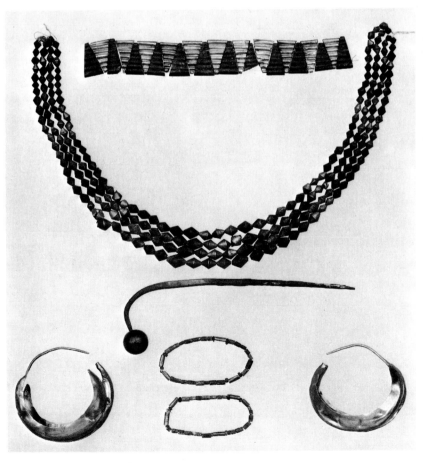

Crushed beneath the weight of the earth, the skull of this Sumerian lady-in-waiting is still adorned with the headdress she wore into the death pit at Ur.

Strands of beads, bracelets, and a pair of earrings completed the costume of a well-dressed Sumerian woman. Curved stickpins held her garments in place.

Rebekah

When Rebekah volunteered to water the camels of Abraham's servant as well as to give the servant a drink, it was a clear sign of answer to prayer. Rebekah's willingness to leave her home to marry a man she had never met is further evidence of the faith and courage of this woman God chose to be Isaac's bride.

The waterpot shown here is from the time of this story, and from the region in which it took place.

Rebekah Goes to Isaac
From Genesis 24:34-67

"I am Abraham's servant," the man told Laban and his family. "The Lord has greatly blessed my master and has made him rich with flocks, herds, silver, and gold, with servants and maids, camels and donkeys.

"Sarah and Abraham had a son when they were very old and Abraham has given him all that he has. But Abraham made me swear that his son would not marry a daughter of the Canaanites in whose land he lives, but that I should go to his family to search for a wife for him.

"I asked him, 'What if the woman will not come with me?' He said, 'The Lord, before Whom I walk, will send His angel with you to make your journey successful. You will bring my son a wife from my family. If they will not give you one, you are freed from my oath.'

"Today when I came to the well I prayed, 'O Lord, the God of my master Abraham, if You are to make my journey successful, show me in this manner. I will stand here by the well as the young women come to draw water. When I ask for a drink, let the one You have chosen also offer to water my camels.'

"Before I had finished praying, Rebekah came out with the jar on her shoulder and went to draw water at the well. I asked her for a drink, and she quickly took the jar from her shoulder and offered to water my camels also. So I drank and she watered my camels.

A young Bedouin woman still relies upon her father to arrange a proper marriage for her.

Although it has kept its ancient name, the city of Haran has dwindled to a small mud-brick village.

The camel on the right is bedecked for a Bedouin bride.

"When I asked her whose daughter she was, she answered, 'The daughter of Bethuel, son of Nahor and Milcah.' Then I put the ring on her nose and the bracelets on her wrists.

"I bowed down and worshiped the Lord and praised Him for leading me in the right way to the daughter of my master's family. Now tell me if you will deal kindly and fairly with my master so that I may know which way to turn."

Laban and Bethuel answered, "How can we speak for it or against it since this matter has come from the Lord? Rebekah is here with us. You may take her with you to be the wife of Abraham's son, as the Lord has spoken."

When Abraham's servant heard that, he bowed to the ground before the Lord. Then he gave Rebekah gifts of silver and gold and garments. He also gave beautiful gifts to Rebekah's mother and to Laban. Then the servant and the men with him ate and drank and spent the night with Rebekah's family.

The next morning the servant was ready to leave. "Send me on my way," he requested.

But Rebekah's mother and brother said, "Let her stay with us a while longer, perhaps ten days. Then she may go."

"Please don't delay me, for the Lord has made my journey successful," the servant told them. "Let me go back to my master immediately."

"Let us ask Rebekah," they replied. "We will see what she wants to do."

When they asked her, Rebekah said, "I will go now."

Eliezer showered Rebekah with a generous dowry of silver and gold jewelry. The old servant also brought rich gifts for the family of the bride.

Isaac was in the fields when Eliezer arrived at the camp with his new bride.

Thus they sent Rebekah and her nurse with the servant and his men. They blessed Rebekah with this blessing:

"You are our sister.
May you become the mother
Of thousands of ten thousands;
May your descendants possess
The gate of their enemies."

Then Rebekah and her servant girls mounted the camels and followed Abraham's servant.

Isaac, who was living in the Negeb at the time, had come for a visit to Beer-lahai-roi. One evening he was walking in a field to meditate. As he looked up, he saw camels coming.

When Rebekah saw Isaac she dismounted from her camel. "Who is that man walking in the field toward us?" she asked.

"My master's son!" the servant answered. So Rebekah covered her face with her veil. Then the servant told Isaac the things that had happened.

Isaac brought Rebekah to his mother Sarah's tent, and she became his wife. He loved Rebekah greatly, and she was a great comfort to him after his mother's death.

BIBLE FOR DAILY LIVING

Bible Truth in Action

"How can we speak for it or against it since this matter has come from the Lord?" Laban and Bethuel told Abraham's servant Eliezer. This was their answer to Eliezer's proposal that Rebekah marry Isaac, whom she and her family had never seen. There is a truth here important for each of us today. When we are convinced that something has been determined by the Lord, how can we be against it? And what further need is there to argue for it? To argue against something the Lord has already determined to do is to argue against the Lord. To continue to argue for it, is to mock the finality of the Lord's decision.

People Profiles

From the incident of this and the preceding reading, draw up a profile for Eliezer. List the qualities of character which are evident from the things he did and the words he spoke. Test this profile with: (1) his loyalty to Abraham, his master; (2) his faithfulness to the Lord; (3) his desire to fulfil his mission; (4) his interest in putting business before the pleasure of eating; (5) his prayerfulness; (6) his gratitude to the Lord for His answer to prayer; (7) his carefulness to fulfil good manners to his host and hostess. Would you trust Eliezer with your business or your household affairs? Do you think Eliezer would make a good leader in your church?

Among the Bedouin tribes a man's wealth is measured by the size of his herds. The welfare of the flocks is his first concern. The three photos below show flocks grazing in the fields near Haran.

Marriage Plans in Bible Times

In most modern countries men and women choose their own marriage partners. But in Bible times parents selected whom the young people would marry.

In Bible times young people relied on their parents' judgment to arrange a suitable marriage for them. Sometimes the wedding plans were made when the bride and groom were still children.

Marriage was more than a bond between husband and wife. When a man and woman married in Bible times, their families became allies. Ancient kings often sealed treaties with marriages between their households.

In return for the loss of his daughter, the groom presented the father of the bride with a present called a "mohar." It could be a gift of money, a piece of land or an offer of special services.

Often a man did not see his wife's face until after they were married, but from be-hind her veil the bride could observe her future husband. She would already know of his generosity through the gifts of clothing and jewelry he gave to her before their marriage.

When all of the arrangements were made and the parents of the bride and groom had settled on the price of the mohar, the couple was officially betrothed. Once the bride and groom were betrothed they were considered legally married even though the wedding feast might be delayed for almost a year. In ancient times this "engagement" was a binding contract that could only be broken by a divorce.

The wedding feast was a joyous celebration that often lasted as long as two weeks. Dressed in his best, escorted by singing and dancing friends, the groom went to the bride's house to claim his new wife. The entire party then returned to the groom's home, where everyone took part in the wedding banquet.

Twin Sons

Isaac and Rebekah had twin sons, named Esau and Jacob. At their birth God announced that the younger Jacob, would inherit the promises made to Abraham. We can perhaps see why in a story of Esau's contempt for God and His promises. One day when hungry, Esau traded away his eldest-son birthright for a bowl of lentil stew!

Esau Sells His Birthright
From Genesis 25

Later Abraham married a woman named Keturah, and she had the following children by him: Zimran, Jokshan, Medan, Midian, Ishbak, and Shuah. Jokshan later had two sons named Sheba and Dedan. Dedan's sons were Asshurim, Letushim, and Leummim. Midian had the following five sons: Ephah, Epher, Hanoch, Abida, and Eldaah.

Abraham gave all that he had to Isaac, but while he was still living he gave gifts to the sons of his concubines and sent them eastward, where they would be far away from Isaac.

Abraham lived to be a hundred and seventy-five. When he breathed his last, he was an old man who had enjoyed a long and satisfying life. Isaac and Ishmael buried him in the cave of Machpelah, near Mamre, in the field of Ephron, the son of

Mournfully Isaac leaves his father's bedside to order the preparations for Abraham's funeral.

Abraham lived his life as a stranger in this land, but he had faith in God's promises that someday it would belong to his descendants. The scene below is the Negeb, near Solomon's mines.

Zohar the Hittite, the field Abraham had bought from the Hittites. Abraham was buried there with his wife Sarah.

After Abraham's death, God's blessings came upon Isaac, who had moved to Beer-lahai-roi. Meanwhile Ishmael, the son of Abraham and Hagar the Egyptian, Sarah's maid, had twelve sons: Nebaioth, Kedar, Abdeel, Mibsam, Mishma, Dumah, Massa, Hadad, Tema, Jetur, Naphish, and Kedemah. These twelve sons founded twelve tribes that bore the names of the twelve princes. Ishmael lived to be a hundred and thirty-seven before he died, and he was buried with his ancestors. His descendants lived throughout the country from Havilah to Shur, which is east of Egypt as a caravan heads toward Assyria, but they were always quarreling with one another.

Isaac was forty years old when he married Rebekah. Because Rebekah could not have children, Isaac begged the Lord for a child. At last Rebekah conceived, but the children struggled within her.

"If they are fighting inside me, why?" Rebekah wondered. So she asked the Lord about it.

The Lord told her:

"Two sons struggle within you,
And two nations shall come forth;

Inside the tent Bedouin men and women live separate lives. A goat's-hair curtain divides the females' quarters from the men's section.

One will be stronger than the other
And the older shall serve the younger."

At last the twins were born. One was red and hairy, with skin like a coat of red hair, and they called him Esau. The other was born with his hand holding Esau's heel, so they named him Jacob, which meant "Someone Who Takes Another's Place." Isaac was sixty at this time.

As Esau and Jacob grew to be young men, Esau became a great hunter. Jacob preferred to stay around the tents, leading a more peaceful life. Isaac favored Esau because he enjoyed the taste of the wild game Esau brought back. But Rebekah favored Jacob.

One time Jacob had cooked some stew when Esau came back hungry from a hunting trip. "I'm famished!" Esau said. "Give me some of that red stuff you're cooking." Because of his remark about "red stuff" he was nicknamed Edom, which meant "Red."

"I'll trade some for your birthright," Jacob answered.

"What good is a birthright to me when I'm dying of hunger?" Esau replied.

"Swear it to me first," said Jacob. So Esau swore this to Jacob and sold his birthright to him.

Jacob then gave Esau bread and lentil stew. When he ate and drank all he wanted, Esau went on his way. Thus Esau showed how little he thought of his birthright.

In a scene familiar to the herdsman, a doe gently nuzzles her kid. This ivory carving dates back to the eighth century B.C.

The delicious smell of Jacob's stew greeted Esau when he returned from a long day of hunting in the fields.

BIBLE FOR DAILY LIVING

Bible Quiz

The latter part of Abraham's life, and the early part of Isaac's life, are covered in this Bible quiz:

1. The man who looked for a bride for Isaac was Abraham's servant
   a. Nahor   b. Laban   c. Eliezer
2. Isaac's bride was
   a. Rachel   b. Rebekah
3. Rebekah was the daughter of
   a. Nahor   b. Abraham   c. Bethuel
4. Rebekah's brother was
   a. Nahor   b. Laban   c. Eliezer
5. Abraham lived to be how old?
   a. 100   b. 137   c. 175
6. Abraham was buried at the cave at
   a. Machpelah   b. Bethlehem   c. Jerusalem
7. Abraham's son Ishmael had how many sons?
   a. 3   b. 7   c. 12
8. Rebekah's two sons were Jacob and
   a. Isaac   b. Esau   c. Bethuel
9. When Isaac married Rebekah, he was how old?
   a. 20   b. 40   c. 60
10. How old was he when his twin sons were born?
    a. 20   b. 40   c. 60
11. Which twin sold his birthright to the other for lentil stew?
    a. Jacob   b. Esau

Answers: 1c, 2b, 3c, 4b, 5c, 6a, 7c, 8b, 9b, 10c, 11b

The Family of Abraham

In the ancient Near East, members within a family often married. This kept property within the family and bound its members more closely together. Abraham's marriage to his half sister Sarah was not an uncommon event.

For many years Abraham and Sarah had no children. Believing she could not have a child of her own, Sarah gave her maid Hagar to Abraham as a wife. Although she bore Ishmael, he was not the child God had promised. Isaac was the "miracle-baby" born to Abraham and Sarah in their old age, and through him and his descendants God created the nation of Israel.

But the Jewish people were not the only nation to grow out of the family of Abraham. The Arab nations trace their origin to Abraham through Ishmael. The Midianites also descended from him through Keturah, Abraham's wife after Sarah's death.

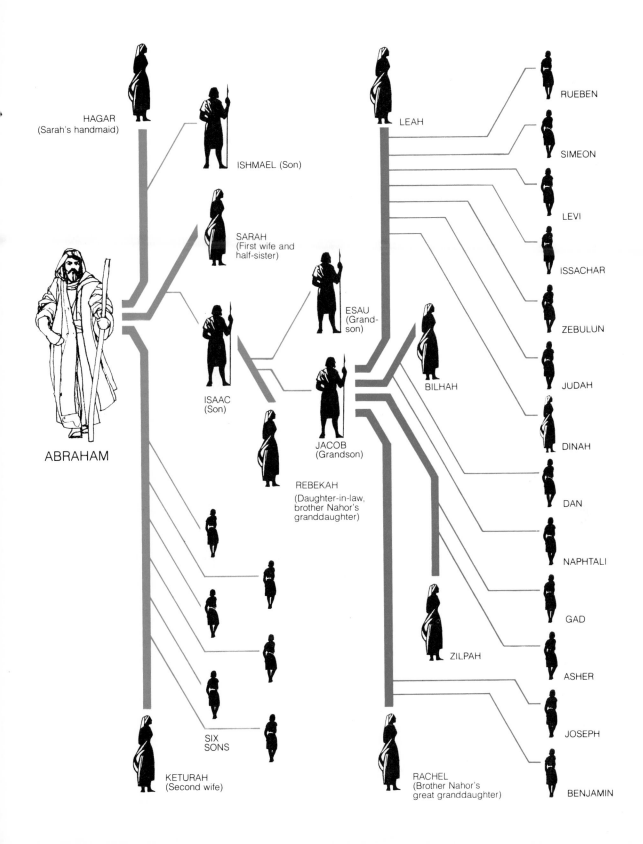

HAGAR
(Sarah's handmaid)

ISHMAEL (Son)

SARAH
(First wife and
half-sister)

ESAU
(Grand-
son)

ISAAC
(Son)

JACOB
(Grandson)

REBEKAH
(Daughter-in-law,
brother Nahor's
granddaughter)

SIX
SONS

KETURAH
(Second wife)

ABRAHAM

LEAH

BILHAH

ZILPAH

RACHEL
(Brother Nahor's
great granddaughter)

RUEBEN

SIMEON

LEVI

ISSACHAR

ZEBULUN

JUDAH

DINAH

DAN

NAPHTALI

GAD

ASHER

JOSEPH

BENJAMIN

Wells

Like his father, Abraham, Isaac was a wanderer. Traveling with great herds, Isaac often came into conflict with the people who were settled in the land. One cause of conflict was water. Water was a life or death issue to the people of the land and their flocks. No wonder Isaac faced growing hostility over wells like those pictured here.

Isaac Refuses to Quarrel
From Genesis 26

A famine swept across the land again as it had in the days of Abraham, so Isaac moved to Gerar where Abimelech, the Philistine king, lived. The Lord appeared to Isaac and said, "Do not go to Egypt. Stay here in this land and I will be with you and bless you; for I will give these lands to you and your descendants, and I will renew with you the covenant I made with your father Abraham. Your descendants will become as numerous as the stars and they will inherit this land from Me and become a blessing to all nations on earth. I will do this because Abraham obeyed Me and kept My covenant and My laws."

Isaac's servants dug the well, but the Philistines claimed the water for themselves. To avoid a war with his neighbors, Isaac moved to a different place and dug a new well.

So Isaac remained in Gerar. When the men of Gerar began to ask about his beautiful wife Rebekah, Isaac said, "She is my sister." He was afraid to tell them that she was his wife, for he thought they would kill him to get her.

But one day after Isaac had lived there for some time, King Abimelech looked out of his window and noticed Isaac caressing Rebekah. Abimelech called for Isaac and said, "Now, look here, she is really your wife, isn't she? Why did you tell us that she is your sister?"

"Because I was afraid someone might kill me to get her," Isaac explained.

"But don't you realize what you have done to us?" Abimelech complained. "One of our men might have lain with her and you would have brought great trouble to us." Then Abimelech proclaimed publicly, "Anyone who harms this man or his wife shall be put to death."

The crops that Isaac sowed that year brought forth rich harvests, a hundred times what he had sown. The Lord blessed him and gave him more and more until Isaac became a wealthy man. Because he had flocks and herds and a large number of servants, the Philistines began to envy him. Some of them filled his wells with dirt, the wells which Abraham's servants had dug.

"Why don't you go somewhere else to live," Abimelech told Isaac. "You are too powerful to live among us now."

So Isaac moved to the Valley of Gerar and settled there. He cleaned out the wells his father Abraham had dug, which the Philistines had filled with dirt when Abraham died, and he gave the wells the names that Abraham had given them.

But when Isaac's servants dug a new well and found a spring of water, the Philistine shepherds quarreled with them and said, "The water is ours!"

Isaac called that well "Esek" for it spoke of the quarreling. His servants dug another well, but the Philistine shepherds quarreled about that one also. So Isaac named it "Sitnah" which meant "Anger."

Isaac left that well also and dug a third well. This time the Philistines left him alone. Isaac named the third well "Rehoboth," which meant "Room," for he said, "At last the Lord has made room for us all and we shall prosper in the land."

Isaac built an altar and called upon the name of the Lord. Isaac moved his tent to Beer-sheba and dug a well there.

One day the Lord appeared to him. "I am the God of your father Abraham," the Lord said. "Do not fear Me, for I am

Deep wells tap the life-giving water beneath the surface of the earth, but the animals cannot reach it. The shepherd must draw the water with a bucket and offer each animal a drink.

with you and will bless you and multiply your descendants for the sake of My servant Abraham."

One day Abimelech came from Gerar with his adviser Ahuzzath and his army commander Phicol. "Why have you come here to me since you hate me and sent me away from you?" Isaac asked.

"It is clear that the Lord is with you, so we would like to make a covenant between us. You will not harm us as we have not harmed you and have done nothing but good to you and sent you away in peace," they answered. "You are now blessed of the Lord."

Isaac prepared a feast for them and they ate and drank together. Early the next morning they made an oath that they would not harm one another. Then Isaac sent them home in peace.

The same day Isaac's servants brought him good news. "We have found water in the well we were digging," they reported. So Isaac named it Shebah, which referred to the oath. Thus the town is still known as Beer-sheba.

When Esau was forty he married Judith, the daughter of Beeri the Hittite, and Basemath, the daughter of Elon the Hittite. These marriages to ungodly people disturbed Isaac and Rebekah greatly.

This lone Bedouin is surrounded by miles of open wilderness.

At the top are ruins of ancient Beer-sheba, where Abraham once lived.

BIBLE FOR DAILY LIVING

Bible Truth in Action

One man cannot quarrel alone. Two must be willing to keep the quarrel alive. When Isaac's Philistine neighbors started a quarrel, Isaac refused to quarrel with them. When they took a well from him, he refused to fight. Instead, he moved on and dug a new well. This happened not once, but twice. Not until Isaac dug a third well did the Philistines leave him alone. What is the best way to win a quarrel? Perhaps Isaac's way—remain silent and move on about one's business.

Words and Meanings

Look up "quarrel" in a dictionary, especially a dictionary of synonyms. As you list some of the synonyms, think of Isaac and the way he handled the Philistines. Did he: (1) Make an issue of their faults? (2) Argue with them? (3) Let his anger get out of control? (4) Fight back as soon as they began the quarrel? (5) Hold a grudge against them? (6) Try to repay evil for evil?

Personal Checkup

Think about the last quarrel you had with someone. How did it start? What was the issue? Who won it? What was the prize for the one who won it? How did the "defeated" person feel? Now think of that quarrel in relationship to Isaac and his neighbors. Measure it with each of the questions above. When you have done this, ask yourself, "What would I do different now in the light of these things?"

Prayer Pointers

Lord, when friends or neighbors or family members become abrasive, give me wisdom to seek You, that I may turn quietly away and let the would-be quarrel die from lack of fuel.

A gently sloping mound (called a "tell") marks the site of the ancient city. Centuries of building on the layers of earlier generations produced this hill or tell at ancient Beer-sheba. Below: modern Beer-sheba from the north.

Isaac's Family

Isaac was the child of promise, the son through whom God fulfilled His covenant with Abraham. The Bible traces Isaac's life from the prophecy of his birth to the day of his death.

Isaac was a "miracle-baby" born to Abraham when he was one hundred years old. His name meant "Laughter" because Sarah laughed when the angel of the Lord said that she would bear a child in her old age.

But this long-awaited baby was not the only child born to Abraham. Ishmael, his son by Hagar, was Isaac's half brother. As the oldest son in the family, Ishmael had a claim to the birthright. But God chose Isaac to be Abraham's heir. He received his father's blessing and the bulk of his household goods.

Material wealth was only a portion of the inheritance Isaac received from his father. More important was the promise God made to Abraham and extended to Isaac. Through him God created the nation of Israel and a line of kings that climaxed centuries later in the birth of Jesus.

As the child of Abraham's old age and his chosen heir, Isaac held a special place in his father's heart. He returned his father's affection with complete obedience. Isaac willingly accompanied Abraham to Mount Moriah, carrying the fuel for the sacrificial fire. Although he questioned his father about the sacrifice, he did not struggle when Abraham bound him and prepared to offer him on the altar.

As Isaac grew to be a young man he continued to trust his father's guidance. He willingly married Rebekah, the wife chosen for him by Eliezer, Abraham's faithful servant. He did not rebel against his father's wishes by choosing a bride for himself from among the Canaanite women.

Just as he was obedient to his father, Isaac was also obedient to the Lord. He learned to trust God through Abraham's example. On Mount Moriah Isaac witnessed the supreme test of his father's faith. His life was spared only at the last moment by God's intervention. In later years the Lord again intervened in Isaac's life by warning him against entering Egypt. In response to the voice of God, Isaac changed the direction of his travels and remained in Canaan.

But the Bible is honest in presenting Isaac's failings as well as his virtues. He was at fault in his dealings with Abimelech, the Philistine king. Using the same false story that his father once used, Isaac pretended that Rebekah was his sister rather than his wife.

Isaac's domestic troubles were also provoked by the favoritism he openly displayed for one son over another. He preferred Esau, the rugged hunter, over Jacob, his younger son. Isaac's obvious preference forced Jacob to gain his father's blessing by dishonesty and deceit. When Esau discovered that he had lost the birthright to his younger brother, his desire for revenge split the family in two.

The strife within his family must have troubled Isaac. By nature he was a peaceful man who avoided conflict with his neighbors. When the Philistine shepherds questioned his right to the wells dug on their land, he moved on and dug new wells for his herds.

In spite of the hostility of the Philistines, Isaac continued to prosper in the land of Canaan. He acquired great herds and a large household that was the envy of his neighbors.

Isaac lived a very long life. Although his eyesight dimmed greatly in his old age, he still enjoyed the respect accorded a man of many years. He lived to see Jacob, his estranged son, return to Canaan as the head of a large family. Before his death he was comforted to know that Jacob and Esau had made peace with one another and the old quarrel between them was forgotten.

Together, Isaac's two sons laid him to rest in the tomb of his father Abraham.

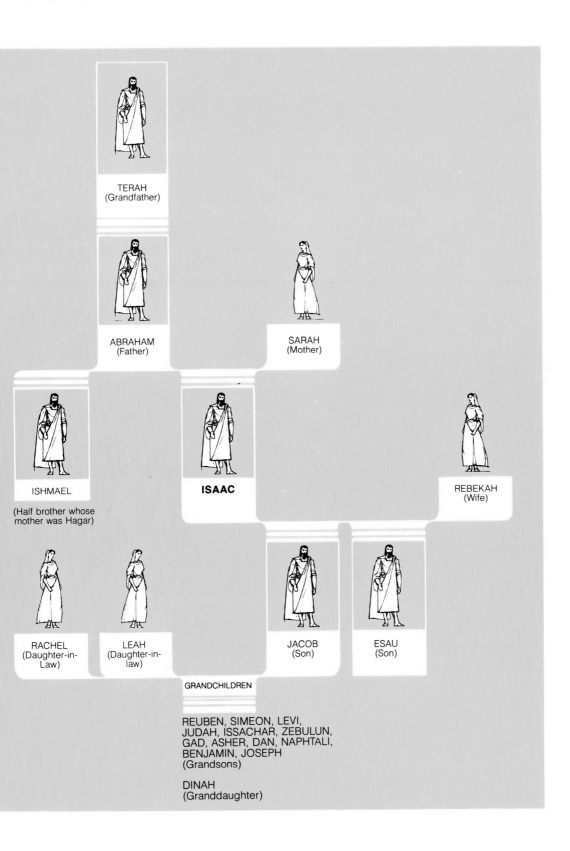

TERAH
(Grandfather)

ABRAHAM
(Father)

SARAH
(Mother)

ISHMAEL

(Half brother whose
mother was Hagar)

ISAAC

REBEKAH
(Wife)

RACHEL
(Daughter-in-
Law)

LEAH
(Daughter-in-
law)

JACOB
(Son)

ESAU
(Son)

GRANDCHILDREN

REUBEN, SIMEON, LEVI,
JUDAH, ISSACHAR, ZEBULUN,
GAD, ASHER, DAN, NAPHTALI,
BENJAMIN, JOSEPH
(Grandsons)

DINAH
(Granddaughter)

How to Use
The Book of Life Program

Through THE BOOK OF LIFE program, you will discover the Bible as a living book, filled with meaning for your life today. The Bible, a book too often veiled by the passage of time and the changing of cultures, will become clear and understandable as never before.

You may wish to approach the Bible through THE BOOK OF LIFE program in your own particular way, and for your own special purpose. In addition, you may wish to use THE BOOK OF LIFE program in one of the following ways, adapting it to your own needs:

1. *Through the Bible*
Too often we focus our attention on the individual events, persons, or facts concerning the Bible, without seeing them as parts of the whole. THE BOOK OF LIFE program will take you on a fascinating journey through the Bible, helping you see a panoramic view from beginning to end. People and events will fit into place in the order in which they appear in the Bible.

2. *Topical*
Approaching the Bible topically is a valuable exercise, for it helps us see a topic as a thread running throughout the Bible, touching many people and many times. Topics of interest are clearly seen in THE BOOK OF LIFE program, both in words and in pictures.

3. *Devotional*
You will appreciate THE BOOK OF LIFE program for devotional purposes. It offers opportunities for a personal encounter with the Lord, and helps you discover a richer prayer life, a clearer understanding of discipleship, a strengthening of faith, and help in exercising the gifts which God has given you.

4. *Personal problem solving*
When personal problems arise, we are anxious to find a resource which will guide us effectively and easily to the answers found in the Scriptures. THE BOOK OF LIFE program gives you that help, as well as guidance in applying what you discover to your daily life.

5. Bible teachings

THE BOOK OF LIFE program is a valuable aid for all who explore the Bible for its teachings. Ministers will appreciate this help for sermon preparation, counseling, and personal study. Others, such as students and teachers at all levels, will find the program useful as they search the Scriptures.

6. Bible personalities

An acquaintance with Bible people and their personal characteristics is a helpful approach to Bible discovery. To understand the Bible adequately, we must first understand the people with whom God worked and how they lived and thought. In moving through the Bible, THE BOOK OF LIFE program focuses on the people of the Bible in the order in which they appear.

7. The Bible setting

The setting in which people and events of the Bible were situated is important in understanding the Bible. THE BOOK OF LIFE program helps you enter into this setting to see clearly the customs and culture of the times, the land and its peoples, and the daily lifestyle of these people. Bible setting is presented in words and expressions which are clearly understood, and in thousands of pictures produced for that purpose. You will return to Bible times and places to experience things as they were.

As you single out one of the ways above, you may use it for personal Bible discovery, for family use, or for Bible study groups, or you may wish to use THE BOOK OF LIFE program as a reference aid.

Many have formed a daily habit of reading the Bible and THE BOOK OF LIFE program in a specific time and place. Others have found it more helpful to do this in a less structured way. But for all, it is well to remember that the Bible is a book to be read for profit and for personal enjoyment. THE BOOK OF LIFE program adds immeasurably to the personal value you receive as you approach the Bible in the way you find most helpful.

A Panoramic View of the Bible / THE BOOK OF LIFE presents a panoramic view of the entire Bible narrative, outlined below volume by volume:

VOLUME 1
God's Pioneers

God creates all things
Adam and Eve are tempted
    and fall
Noah builds an ark for the Flood
Some men build a tower at Babel
Abraham moves from Ur
God makes a covenant
    with Abraham
Sodom is destroyed
Abraham offers Isaac
Isaac marries Rebekah and they
    have Jacob and Esau

VOLUME 2
A Chosen People

Jacob deceives Isaac
Jacob dreams of a ladder
At Haran, Jacob marries Rachel
    and Leah, and has twelve sons
Jacob returns to Canaan
Joseph is sold as a slave, and is
    made governor of Egypt
Jacob and his family move
    to Egypt

VOLUME 3
Exodus from Bondage

Jacob's descendants become
    slaves in Egypt
Moses is adopted by
    Pharaoh's daughter
Moses sees a burning bush
God sends ten plagues
The Israelites leave Egypt
    and cross the Red Sea
God gives manna, water,
    and His law, with
    the Ten Commandments,
    in the wilderness

VOLUME 4
God's Tabernacle

God gives blueprints for
    the tabernacle
God sets up the priesthood
The Israelites make a golden calf
The tablets of stone are broken
    and God replaces them
The tabernacle is built
Aaron and his sons
    become priests

VOLUME 5
God's Laws

The Israelites are numbered
The Levites are consecrated
God sends a plague with quail
Spies go into the Promised Land;
    the people refuse to enter
    and are forced to stay
    in the wilderness
Korah rebels
A bronze serpent is set up

VOLUME 6
Wilderness Wanderings

King Balak sends for Balaam
Balaam blesses Israel
Offerings are established for
    festal seasons
The tribes of Reuben and Gad
    settle in Gilead
Plans are made for the conquest
    of Canaan
Levitical cities and cities of
    refuge are established
Moses dies

VOLUME 7
The Promised Land

Spies scout Canaan
The Israelites cross the
    Jordan River
The Israelites conquer Jericho
    and Ai
Gibeonites trick Joshua
The sun and moon stand still
Hebron is given to Caleb
The land is divided among
    the tribes
Joshua dies

VOLUME 8
The Judges

Deborah and Barak win a battle
Gideon tests God with a fleece;
    his three hundred win a battle
Jephthah makes a foolish vow
Samson gets into trouble with
    Delilah and other Philistines
The Danites move northward
The tribe of Benjamin is almost
    destroyed
Ruth moves to Bethlehem
    and marries Boaz

VOLUME 9
The Nation Unites

Samuel is born and lives
    at the tabernacle
God calls Samuel
The Ark is captured
Samuel serves as judge
Saul becomes king
David is anointed
David fights Goliath
Jonathan and David become
    friends

VOLUME 10
The Warrior King

David hides from King Saul
Samuel dies
David lives with the Philistines
Saul dies
David becomes king
David marries Bath-sheba
David leads Israel in many wars

VOLUME 11
Israel's Golden Age

The Ark is returned to Israel
David plans to build a temple
David is kind to Mephibosheth
Absalom rebels against David
David numbers his people
Preparations are made to build
    the temple
Solomon becomes king

VOLUME 12
The Nation Divides

King David dies
Solomon rules as a wise king
Solomon builds the temple
Solomon becomes rich
    and famous
The queen of Sheba visits
    Solomon
Rehoboam becomes king and
    the ten tribes revolt
The nation divides into Judah
    and Israel, ruled by
    numerous kings